Divine H  Guaran

Seven Undisputable Truths That Prove That Divine Healing Is Guaranteed To Every Believer

By Troy J. Edwards

Divine Healing: Guaranteed by Troy J. Edwards

Copyright (c) 1997 by Troy J. Edwards

Published by **Victorious Word Christian Fellowship**

Contents

Introduction   5

1. It Is Always God's Will to Heal   7
2. It Is God's Desire to Heal You   15
3. Jesus Bore Your Sicknesses and Disease   25
4. Sickness Is the Result of Sin, Therefore Healing Must
       Accompany Forgiveness   35
5. Satan: The Source of Sickness   45
6. Healing: Your Covenant Right   57
7. Healing Glorifies God   69
8. How to Appropriate Healing   79
9. How to Minister Healing To the Sick   89
10. Practical Wisdom and Divine Healing   99

Appendix One: Healing Promises   109
Insert: Seven Reasons Why You Can Trust God for Healing   113
Notes   115
Invitation for Salvation and Baptism with the Holy Spirit   119

This book is dedicated to all of God's Children who love God and desire the best that He has for them.

Introduction

"So God's blessings are given to us by faith, as a free gift; WE ARE CERTAIN TO GET THEM ...." (Rom. 4:16)

The church has understood for years that all of God's blessings were free. The part that many of us have failed to understand is the CERTAINTY of God's blessings.

Although God is generous, faith is not so much established upon the generosity of God as it is upon His integrity. Our faith is not grounded in the fact that God's promises are free as it is in the fact that they are SURE to every believer and that they are GUARANTEED.

So many believers have the hardest struggle when it comes to God's blessing of divine healing. When one's body is wracked with pain it is very hard to stand in faith if you are not CERTAIN that God will heal you. The last thing a person needs is a theological discourse on why God does not heal today or why He may choose to heal others but not you.

It is when we are sure that God will heal (or has healed) that we are able to stand in the midst of trials and tribulations and contradicting circumstance. It is the guarantee that God will do it (or has done it) that enables us to be patient and endure.

This book is written to establish God's people in the CERTAINTY of divine healing. God wants you to know that it is GUARANTEED to you. I did not write this to debate with those who have opposing views. You and I need not waste time trying to prove our points.

I never try to change the hard hearts of others. That is the job of the Holy Spirit. However, I do try to help those who truly want to know what the Scriptures say. I want to help those who will accept God's Word on the subject and who need healing.

If you study the truths presented in this book they will build your faith and you are sure to be healed. It is faith that brings any of

God's blessings into manifestation in our lives. This book was designed to get your faith working in the area of healing.

I encourage you to meditate on what God's Word has to say about this important subject. You will find that you need not ever again accept sickness in your life or in that of your family members.

Chapter One

It Is Always God's Will To Heal You

"So God's blessings are given to us by faith, as a free gift; WE ARE CERTAIN TO GET THEM ...." (Rom. 4:16; The Living Bible)

I believe that many of us have read in the Bible what we believe to be instant healings. Others have been to meetings, churches, or have seen television programs where an evangelist will call out a sickness and the person gets instantly healed. Sometimes we have seen that a person will have hands laid upon them by a great man of God and "whammo," God heals them at a snap of the finger.

All of us would like to receive our healing that way. However, God does not always choose to operate that way. The most common way that God has chosen to heal His people is by faith in His promises. The gift of healings operates as the Spirit wills (1 Cor. 12:11). It is obvious that He does not always "will" to operate that gift. However, God always "wills" to heal.

Appropriating healing by faith in God's promises is THE BEST WAY to receive it. Many have been healed through the gifts only to lose what they had because they did not know what the Word said concerning it. The devil loves an ignorant Christian. He can easily steal from them.

Many years ago while sitting in church I was experiencing sharp pains in my back. At the end of the service the Spirit of God moved upon the pastor and he began to operate in the gift of healings. At first he commanded all headaches to be healed in Jesus name - and they were. He commanded several other minor ailments to be healed and it happened. As I anxiously waited, he finally commanded the healing of all backaches and the pain in my back left instantly. I was excited and overjoyed (not to mention relieved).

Three days later that same pain returned to my back. It wasn't because I did not believe in healing nor did I doubt that I had been healed. It was because I lacked a very important element called "faith." I did not ground myself in the Scriptures concerning health and healing and I therefore allowed Satan to steal God's blessing from me. The Bible tells us that we are destroyed for a lack of knowledge (Hosea 4:6).

Faith is the key to guarantee divine healing in your body. Yet people have a problem with two things. If it doesn't happen instantly they discontinue EXERCISING faith and they either allow Satan to make them think that they have NO faith or that it was never God's will to heal them anyway.

The other thing is that there are still many today that oppose healing for some reason or another. Their views are printed in major Christian magazines, periodicals, books, commentaries, and even some study Bibles. Many Christians who read these publications are confused concerning this issue. God is not the author of confusion but of peace (1 Cor. 14:33).

I will show you seven indisputable truths from the Bible concerning divine healing that will strengthen your faith. It will take faith to appropriate the healing God has made available to you. This faith can only come by hearing and hearing by the Word of God (Rom. 10:17).

If you will read these truths carefully and meditate upon them, you will find yourself being strengthened in your inner man. This will result in the supernatural power of God manifesting itself upon the outer man.

Allow me to present three common views concerning divine healing held by various groups in the body of Christ:

A. Healing is not for today. This miracle only belonged to the apostolic age until the full canon of scripture was written. Then God withdrew His healing power. Today God has given us doctors with much knowledge to help us.

B. God MAY heal today IF it is His will. Notice the key words "may" and "if." He is certainly able but it may not be His will to heal everyone. Sometimes He does and sometimes He doesn't. He is sovereign and therefore has the right to decide whom He will heal and whom He will not.

C. It is the will of God to heal all who come to Him. He has provided this healing in the atonement that Christ made by His blood. It is the covenant right of every believer.

The first view is so ludicrous that I will not take a lot of space to deal with it. There is not one shred of scriptural evidence that can be used to prove that healing or any other miracle was withdrawn from the church. On the contrary there is all the evidence today to prove the opposite. Scripture and experience show us that God is still healing and performing all kinds of other signs and wonders today.

Those who oppose healing and the miraculous in the church today will attribute any manifestation of these things to the devil. If the devil has become more powerful than God then perhaps we are on the wrong side. However, I think not. Satan does work false miracles today. **But in order to have a fake then there must be a genuine.** You cannot counterfeit three dollar bills because there are not any. Satan can only COPY what he has seen God do. He has not been able to come up with an original idea in all of these centuries. Therefore, the very idea that all healings and miracles are satanic brings a person on the borderline of blasphemy against the Holy Spirit (Matt. 12:24-32).

The second view is more deceptive and has kept more people from their healing than the first one. This view is even being taught today in many so called Charismatic fellowships. There is much twisting of Scripture to prove this view and we will look at some of them.

One must read the Bible with a clear mind that is free from the bias that many of today's scholars and theologians teach. Only then will we be able to interpret the God's promises for what they really mean.

The Bible makes it very clear that it is God's will to heal everyone. He shows us in His Word that He is no respecter of persons:

"And ye masters, do the same things unto them, forbearing threatening; knowing that your master also is in heaven; NEITHER IS THERE RESPECT OF PERSONS WITH HIM" (Eph. 6:9)

The Everyday Bible translates the latter part of that verse this way: *"And that Master treats everyone alike."* The NIV says it this way: *".....and there is NO FAVORITISM with him."* This applies to healing as well as everything else. If God is going about healing some of His children and not healing others then He is playing favorites and He is violating His own Word. Yet we know that this could not be true.

The book of Acts has a similar statement:

"Then Peter opened his mouth, and said, of a truth I perceive that God is no respecter of persons:" (Acts 10:34)

The Jewish New Testament translates it this way: *"I now understand that God does not play favorites."* What I like about this statement in Acts is that it is directly linked to the healing ministry of Jesus. Four verses down in the same chapter we read:

"How God anointed Jesus of Nazareth with the Holy Ghost and with power: who went about doing good, and healing ALL that were oppressed of the devil; for God was with him." (Acts 10:38)

What He will do for one He will do for all. Peter first laid the principle to the leaders of the Jewish church that God plays no favorites among people concerning any of His salvation benefits. Then He illustrates this point by reminding them of how Jesus healed "ALL," not just a few, who were under Satan's oppression of sickness.

There are many instances in the gospels that tell us that when Jesus healed, He healed ALL:

*"When the even was come, they brought unto him many that were possessed with devils: and he cast out the spirits with his word, AND HEALED **ALL** THAT WERE SICK: That it might be fulfilled which was spoken by Essays the prophet, saying, Himself took our infirmities, and bare our sicknesses."* (Matt. 8:16-17; see also Matt. 4:24; 12:15; Mark 1:32; Luke 4:40; 6:19).

Jesus healed **all** because it was prophesied by Isaiah that His healing would be available to all through His atonement on our behalf. Most Bible scholars have no problem believing that the atonement provides salvation for ALL. They have no trouble believing that it is the will of God that ALL be saved (1 Tim. 2:4; 2 Pet. 3:9). Nevertheless, the same Bible makes it clear that Healing, as salvation, is for all.

The only thing that our opponents have to prove their case against our teaching that "healing is for all" are a few misquoted Scripture and cases of people that they knew who were good Christians but died sick. Yet we all know of good people who have died and have gone to hell. Does that prove that salvation is not for all? Certainly not.

Furthermore, if God was the type who picked and chose whom He was going to heal then there would never be an instance in Scripture that says He healed ALL. It would say "and Jesus healed many but only those for whom it was God's will." The only time Jesus did not heal all was when there was unbelief present (Matt. 13:58).

The Bible shows individual instances of people who came to Jesus for healing. All of those recorded shows that faith was displayed and healing was appropriated. Not one time did He tell any of them, "Sorry, I know you have faith but it just isn't my Father's will to heal you." No. They all received healing. Their faith had to come from somewhere. Obviously every one of these people knew that it was God's will to heal them or they would not have come to Jesus in the first place. <u>You can only have faith if you know the will of God.</u>

These Scriptures prove that it is God's will to heal because Jesus did ONLY the will of His Father:

> *"I can of my own self do nothing: as I hear, I judge: and my judgement is just; because I seek not mine own will, but the will of the Father which sent me."* (John 5:30).

Therefore, Jesus came to earth demonstrating the will of God for all mankind. All that He ever said and did was from the Father (John 12:49, 50; 14:9, 10, 24) and was recorded in the Bible for our benefit.

The will of our Father is the same in heaven as it is on earth. He taught us to pray, *"Thy kingdom come, thy will be done in earth, as it is in heaven."* (Matt. 6:10). If Jesus taught us to pray this way then surely we would expect God to answer such a prayer. Jesus would not have us pray something that God was not willing to do. God wants His will done on earth just as it is done in heaven. Let's look at something the Bible says about heaven:

> *"In the midst of the street of it, and on either side of the river, was there the tree of life, which bare twelve manner of fruits, and yielded her fruit every month: and the leaves were for the HEALING of the nations. And there shall be NO MORE CURSE...."* (Rev. 22:2, 3)

Sickness and disease are included in the curse (Deut. 28). This curse does not exist in heaven. Only healing and health exists. So we can see that God's will for us is revealed in heaven. If sickness was His will then there would be sickness in heaven. Nevertheless, there isn't. Therefore it cannot be His will for you and I who are citizens of heaven to be sick (Eph. 2:6; 3:15; Phil. 3:20; Col. 1:13).

If that were not enough, the Bible gives us Scripture that shows definite proof that it is God's will to heal:

*"Is anyone among you sick? Let him call for the elders of the church, and let them pray over him, anointing him with oil in the name of the Lord. And the prayer of faith **WILL** save the sick, and the Lord **WILL** raise him up."* (James 5:14-15; NKJV).

This passage leaves no question as to what God will do if this passage is applied. God has made provision for healing and will release it into our physical bodies when the prayer of faith is prayed. Faith comes by hearing and hearing by the Word of God. A person's word reveals their will. God's word reveals His will concerning healing and that will is what gives us faith to pray the prayer of faith. So the prayer of faith is simply praying the revealed will of God as shown in His Word.

Nonetheless, many theologians and Bible scholars will go out of their way to twist the meaning of this verse. One man used God's sovereignty as an excuse to say that if He chooses not to heal then He will not. If God does not heal then this passage is a lie because it says that He WILL do it. If we cannot believe this passage how can we believe any of the others? How can we believe the ones that tell us we are saved on our way to heaven?

Make no mistake about it, ALL of God's word is truth (John 17:17). God would not lie in any part of it. God does not even change His mind concerning any portion of His Word and that includes Healing (Num. 23:19; Mal. 3:6; Heb. 6:17-18; 13:8). God has made provision for healing and we know that it is His will. Let's look at one more passage of Scripture to prove this point:

*"And He said to them, 'Go into all the world and preach the gospel to every creature......And these signs will follow those who believe.....they **WILL** lay hands on the sick and they WILL recover.'"* (Mark 16:15, 17, 18; NKJV)

Notice that in James and Mark the word *"will"* is used concerning the healing of the sick. It leaves no room for doubt. The words "might, maybe, or if it be my will" are not used here. These words are only additions made by unbelieving preachers who desire to defend their denominational and theological positions.

Some have even gone as far as to say that Mark 16:15-20 are not a part of the original manuscripts and are not for us today. It is true that TWO manuscripts do not contain these passages, however over 4200 Greek manuscripts, many with great authenticity do include them.

If we are going to use this argument to disprove Mark 16 then we must also remember that other very important (and accepted) passages of Scripture are also left out of some of the original manuscripts such as the first 46 chapters of Genesis, Psalms 105-137, and Hebrews 9:14-13:25.

The real truth of the matter is that Satan has always attempted to cast doubt upon the Word of God (Gen. 3:1-5). Unfortunately he has used those who claim to be ministers of the gospel. It is Satan's desire to bring doubt upon God's will concerning your healing. He does this in order to destroy you.

Even if Mark 16:15-20 were not a part of the original manuscripts, we have enough evidence from other passages of Scripture to prove that healing of the sick should accompany the preaching of the gospel (Matt. 10:7-8; Luke 9:1-6; Acts 8:5-8; 14:7-10; Rom. 15:19). God places so much importance on the healing of the sick that He commands it to be done along with the preaching of the gospel. This shows that healing is always the will of God.

When we say that it is always God's will to heal we are talking about His decree and purpose and His purpose for healing. We are talking about what He demands to be done. It is His decree and His purpose that the sick are made well. When we learn what God's Word has to say then we will no longer question the will of God concerning healing. It always has been and always will be the will of God to heal anyone and everyone who comes to Him in faith.

Chapter Two

It Is God's Desire To Heal You

"So God's blessings are given to us by faith, as a free gift; WE ARE CERTAIN TO GET THEM......" (Rom. 4:16; Living Bible)

In these lessons on healing, I am showing you some indisputable truths from the Bible that will strengthen your faith. Healing is for every child of God and none of us should have to tolerate any kind of sickness, disease, handicap, or physical deformity.

But without an understanding of what the Bible has to say concerning the subject, we will continue to allow these things to rule in our lives. All of God's blessing are appropriated by faith and this faith will only come as we know what God's Word says about the things we desire from Him. That is the purpose of teaching these lessons. Healing belongs to you and we want your faith to be strengthened so that you can receive it.

In our last lesson we dealt with the first indisputable truth concerning healing which is that it is ALWAYS God's will to heal. Not just sometimes or not just to a select few but it is always His will to heal.

However, not only is it God's will (His decree and purpose) to heal you, but we will show you that it is also His desire. God wants to heal you.

Some people, and this includes many Christians, seem to have a distorted view of God. They imagine a sadistic God who seems to get pleasure out of His children suffering pain and torment. Many who hold this view think that they are suffering for the kingdom of God when they are sick. Some think that God is using the sickness to teach them a lesson or to work some divine purpose in their life.

It's incredible how Satan has fed these lies to the church and even more incredible how the majority of Christians have accepted them. It seems that we can think in terms of common sense when it comes to natural things but we get very stupid when it comes to the spiritual.

If God is a true Father then why would He want to see His children suffering in pain and torment? Only a child abuser would want that. Are we to compare our heavenly Father to a child abuser.

No one ever questions God's ability to heal. If we did that then we could no longer call Him God. After all the thing that makes Him God is His ability to do anything. If He has this omnipotent power to do anything, don't you think that being a true Father He would desire to use it on behalf of His sick children? Jesus answers this question for us:

> *"And there came a leper to him, beseeching him, and kneeling down to him, and saying unto him, if thou wilt, thou canst make me clean. And Jesus, moved with compassion, put forth his hand, and touched him, and saith unto him, I WILL; be thou clean."* (Mark 1:40-41).

This leper knew that Jesus had the ABILITY to heal. This man like many today was not sure if it was the will of God to receive healing, but then Jesus uses two words, "I will." This revealed God's desire for this man's healing and gave him the faith to receive it.

This verse was recorded so that we too will know that God's desire is for our healing (1 Cor. 10:6; 2 Tim. 3:16; Heb. 6:12). The Bible tells us that there were many miracles that Jesus did but all of them could not be recorded (John 21:25). The Holy Spirit selected some of these many miracles to teach us different lesson and to build our faith.

The Everyday Bible interprets Mark 1:40-42 this way:

> *"A man who had a harmful skin disease came to Jesus. The man fell to his knees and begged Jesus, 'I know that you can heal me if you will.' Jesus felt sorry for the*

man. So he touched him and said, 'I WANT TO HEAL YOU. Be healed!' At once the disease left the man, and he was healed."

The word "want" (or "will" in the KJV) in the Greek means to delight in or to desire to do it. In our last lesson we showed you that Jesus never did His own will but that of His Father. Jesus told Phillip *"he that hath seen me hath seen the Father."* (John 14:9).

Jesus came demonstrating the heart of our Father. When people were sick Jesus was always moved with compassion and always desired to heal their physical bodies (Matt. 14:14; 20:34; Mark 1:41; 5:1-20; Luke 7:11-15). Therefore if Jesus wanted to heal then that means God wanted to heal. If God wanted to heal back then it only stands to reason that He still wants to heal now because He never changes (Mal. 3:6; Heb. 13:8). God is still the compassionate God today that He was yesterday.

In another passage we find that it is God's desire for us to be in good health:

"Beloved, I wish above all things that thou mayest prosper and be in health, even as thy soul prospereth." (3 John 2)

Some unbelieving scholars teach that this was a greeting meant for Gaius only and that it only applied to him. They say that we cannot claim this promise. Yet we must remember that ALL scripture is given by the inspiration of God (2 Tim. 3:16) and John was writing under the inspiration of the Holy Spirit.

The Holy Spirit inspired the Scriptures to be written to reveal to man the heart and will of God for him. This means that John was conveying God's wish for Gaius and every other reader of this epistle. If that were not true then the Holy Spirit would not have inspired John to write this.

Paul wrote epistles to the Ephesians, Galatians, Philippians, and other churches. In them he always included salutations and greetings of grace and peace. Are we not to claim the blessings in these epistles because they were addressed to those particular churches? Paul also included prayers to many of the churches he wrote to under the inspiration of God. Are we not to pray these prayers for ourselves because they were written to some particular church?

I think not. Peter places Paul's epistle in the same category as scripture (2 Pet. 3:15-16). Therefore John's and Peter's epistles are Scripture and ALL scripture is for our profit (2 Tim. 3:16). The wish for health and prosperity are for us as well as for Gaius. God wants us to be healthy and prosper:

> *"Let the Lord be magnified, which hath PLEASURE in the prosperity of his servant."* (Psalm 35:27)

The Everyday Bible quotes Psalm 35:27 this way: *"...He loves to see his servants do well."* The NIV says it this way: *"....who delights in the well-being of his servant."* It pleases and delights God for you and I to do well. He loves to see it. Don't you realize that if God has pleasure in your health and well being and He has the ability to make it happen then HE WILL DO IT?

So many people have been taught just the opposite of this and therefore have a hard time receiving healing even when they begin to learn that it is available to them. Many people do not realize that God wants them to be healed more than they want to.

Allow me to present more Scriptural proof of this. People have been taught for so long that God gets some kind of demented pleasure from seeing His children in pain and suffering. Therefore, we find it necessary to provide you with more faith building proof to show you this is an error.

When Jesus came to earth, His message to the people was the gospel of the kingdom. That is still His message today. The Bible teaches that divine healing and deliverance are part of this kingdom:

> *"And Jesus went about all Galilee, teaching in their synagogues, and preaching the gospel of the kingdom, and **healing all manner of sickness** and all manner of diseases among the people."* (Matt. 4:23)

18

*"And as you go preach, saying, the kingdom of heaven is at hand. **Heal the sick**, cleanse the lepers, raise the dead, cast out devils: freely ye have received, freely give."* (Matt. 10:7-8)

*"And he sent them to preach the kingdom of God, and to **heal the sick**."* (Luke 9:2)

*"And **heal the sick** that are therein, and say unto them, The kingdom of God is come nigh unto you."* (Luke 10:9)

"But if I with the finger of God cast out devils, no doubt the kingdom of God is come upon you." (Luke 11:20)

Deliverance and healing were a physical manifestation of God's kingdom being at hand. He wanted people to know that the kingdom was available to them and all of the kingdom benefits. Now look at what Jesus says about God's desire for us:

*"Fear not little flock; for it is your Father's **GOOD PLEASURE** to give you the kingdom."* (Luke 12:32)

The Everyday Bible interprets it this way: *"Don't fear, little flock. Your Father **WANTS** to give you the kingdom."* I also like the Living Bible's paraphrase: *"So don't be afraid, little flock. For it gives your Father great happiness to give you the kingdom."*

If God wants to give you the kingdom then naturally He wants you to have everything that comes with it. That includes the healing. God wants you healed and healthy. This is His desire for you. He gets great happiness out of it and He gets much pleasure from your healing. Don't you want to make God happy? Then claim your healing in Jesus name. This will please the Father.

The problem has been that we have failed to understand the Father heart of God. Christians have thought of Him more as God then they have as Father. Under the Old Covenant He was God to the people, but in this New Covenant, He is both God and Father to us.

There is not one parent reading this right now who desires to see his or her children sick. When your children get sick you do everything you can to bring them back to health. Some parents would rather take the sickness upon themselves then to watch their child suffer. It's more torturous to watch your own child suffer then for you to be sick yourself.

Many of us would spend thousands, maybe even millions of dollars if we have to in order to bring and keep our children in an acceptable state of health. In other words, we will do all that is in our ability to see that our children our healed. Well, look at what God says about Himself:

> *"If ye then, being evil, know how to give good gifts unto your children, how much more shall your Father which is in heaven give good things to them that ask him?"* (Matt. 7:11)

God compares Himself to earthly fathers. He shows us that if our hearts are for our children then His heart is even greater for His own. We have a sin nature yet we will do our best for our children. God is totally holy and His very nature is love. How could He not do a million times more than the best of earthly Fathers? Especially when His ability to do it exceeds that of man to do for his children.

Notice that this Scripture says that God will give GOOD THINGS to them that ask Him. Is healing a good thing or is sickness a good thing? If you have ever been sick I do not think you honestly thought that it was a good thing. The Bible tells us the exact opposite concerning sickness:

> *"And the Lord will take away from thee all sickness, and will put none of the **EVIL** diseases of Egypt, which thou knowest, upon thee......"* (Deut 7:15)

What is God's description of sickness and disease? It is EVIL. The exact opposite of good is evil.

It's not a good thing for someone to be sick and not be able to work and take care of his or her family. They become a burden to others. Our Father wants us to have GOOD THINGS. The Bible makes it clear that healing is a good thing:

"He sent his word, and HEALED them, and delivered them from their destructions. Oh that men would praise the Lord for his GOODNESS, and his wonderful works to the children of men." (Psalm 107:20-21)

Notice that healing is linked to the goodness of God. This proves that healing is a good thing. Best of all, it's available through God's GOOD WORD (Josh 21:45; 23:14; 1 Kings 8:56; Heb. 6:5).

Acts 10:38 tells that Jesus,

"......went about doing GOOD, and HEALING all that were oppressed of the devil; for God was with him."

The good that Jesus went about doing was HEALING. Again we see from the Bible that healing is a good thing. Our Father wants to give us good things. You need not be afraid to ask God to manifest His healing power in your mortal body. It's a good thing and He wants to give it to you because He loves you.

"At that day ye shall ask in my name: and I say not unto you, that I will pray the Father for you: For THE FATHER HIMSELF LOVETH YOU....." (John 16:26-27)

God loves us so much that He sent Jesus to die on the cross for us so that we can be totally free from all sin, oppression, poverty, and sickness. He has made this available to you and He wants you to have it.

Suppose I left my children a some hard earned money and told them how they can appropriate it. Yet one of my children kept saying, "Maybe dad doesn't really want me to touch that money. Perhaps it's not his will for me to have it right now." Don't you think that it would grieve my heart? I worked hard for that money and from genuine love I gave it to my children. Nevertheless, they choose to entertain such an attitude. How would you feel if your children did that? How would you like to see your children live poverty stricken when you have made a life of abundance available to them?

I really believe that it grieves the heart of our Father when His children question His love or give some perverted definition of His love (i.e. , God loves you, that's why He put that sickness on you. He has some great lesson for you to learn). God has feelings too. He doesn't like a false representation of His character any more than you do.

God WANTS His children healed and He has made every provision through our Lord Jesus Christ for this.

Now that we have established the fact that it is God's desire to heal us the question may come to mind, "Why are some good Christians still sick." Although we will cover some things as we progress in these lessons I want to touch one reason for why healing isn't always manifested.

As we stated in our last lesson, faith is the key that will unlock the healing power of God as well as all of His other kingdom blessings into our lives. God is a gentleman and He will not force anything upon us. Even if it's a good thing.

One night my oldest daughter woke up sick. We prayed for her healing but we knew that she was suffering so we wanted to give her some medicine to relieve the pain until the healing had manifested. She had taken this particular medicine before and did not like the taste of it. As we tried to feed it to her she kept her mouth closed and screamed and cried to prevent it from getting into her mouth. So we gave up.

As much as I desired to see her suffering relieved, she had to accept the provision that we as her parents made available for her.

However she did not trust her parents enough to take the medicine. She refused it and therefore suffered a while longer than she had to.

God has made every provision for our healing and it is His intense desire to give it to us. But if we are going to fight with God about it and misinterpret His promises then of course we will never receive it. Many Christians have either never been taught properly or they just refuse to believe. Either way they remain sick and some die before they should. They leave behind them a grieving family who becomes bitter with God. They are bitter because they wonder "why did God have to take him/her so soon. He/she was so young."

God is not in the business of "taking" anyone. He wants us to live long, healthy and prosperous lives so that we can preach His gospel and draw others into the kingdom.

God does not possess one iota of selfishness. All that He has (and He has much more than we could ever conceive in our minds) He desires to share with those who come to Him in faith. He desires to show the riches of His grace and limitlessness of His goodness to all of His creatures. That is why there is much rejoicing in heaven when a sinner repents (Luke 15:7-10).

The purpose of these lessons is to help you see this truth so that you will never again doubt that healing is for you and that you can appropriate it. For those who may already know this then I am sure that we are teaching this in a way that will increase your faith for this blessing.

Believe that it is God's will that you receive healing. Believe that it is His desire. In our next lesson we will give you the third indisputable truth concerning God's healing for you.

Chapter Three

Jesus Bore Your Sicknesses And Disease

"So God's blessings are given to us by faith, as a free gift; WE ARE CERTAIN TO GET THEM....." (Rom. 4:16; Living Bible)

In these lessons we are attempting to strengthen your faith in the area of divine healing. We want you to know beyond a shadow of a doubt that you can be free from any sickness or disease that may attack your body.

God wants you healed and healthy. It is His divine will for you. Anything less is living below the rights and privileges that have been made available to you.

We are giving you seven indisputable truths concerning divine healing If you will meditate upon the truths you will never again doubt that healing belongs to you.

According to the Bible, Jesus has made an ATONEMENT for your sins and your sicknesses. Atonement means *"to cover, to purge away, reconcile, pardon, pacify, put off."* Myer Pearlman says *"To atone for sin is to cover from God's sight so that it loses its power to provoke wrath."* {1}

An atonement is a SUBSTITUTION. God could not just overlook sin. It had to be punished. Because of God's righteousness and holiness He had to judge it. Because of His grace and mercy He found a means whereby He could judge it and free the sinner from the guilt and the power of sin.

In the Old Testament God used the blood of certain types of animals to atone for the sin of the people (Lev. 4:20-35; 5:6-18; 10:17; 16:10, 11, 17:11). All of these pointed to the ultimate blood sacrifice that would be made by our Lord Jesus Himself (Heb. 2:17; 9:14; Eph. 1:7; Matt. 26:28; Col. 1:20; Rom. 3:25).

The blood of Jesus was more effective in dealing with sin then the blood of animals under the Old Testament. The animals could only deliver one from the penalty of sin. If one sinned again then another sacrifice had to be made. The blood of Jesus not only delivers us from the penalty but also the power of sin. Sin no longer has dominion over us (John 1:7-9; Rom. 6; Rev. 1:5). It is an atonement that continues to cleanse. It need not be made again but it can be continually appropriated.

Under the Old Testament atonement also delivered them from the results of their sin. The results and penalties of sin were sickness, poverty, and defeat. If those whose covenant and whose blood sacrifices were less than what is offered to us had such blessings as healing, prosperity, and victory in all areas of life, should we who are under the New Covenant which is better have those and more (Heb. 8:6)?

Most evangelical teachers have no problems telling us that our sins were covered in the atonement Christ made for us. However, they have serious problems with those who teach that our sicknesses were covered too. Yet if Christ did not deal with the results of sin as well as with sin itself then how can atonement be complete. That's like getting rid of the skunk and leaving the smell. The reason we wanted to get rid of the skunk is because of the smell that it was giving.

Satan does not want people to get the full benefits of Christ's atonement and has deceived religious leaders into propagating lies that will leave you in the bondage of his works. The Scriptures if read literally and with no religious, super spiritual bias, or denominational interpretation, shows us very clearly that Christ's atonement covered our sickness as well as our sins.

"He is despised and rejected of men; a man of sorrows, and acquainted with grief: and we hid as it were [our] faces from him; he was despised, and we esteemed him not. Surely he hath borne our griefs, and carried our sorrows: yet we did esteem him stricken, smitten of God, and afflicted. But he was wounded for our transgressions, he was bruised for our iniquities: the chastisement of our peace was upon him; and with his stripes we are healed." (Isa. 53:3-5)

Notice the word **"surely"** in this passage. It means *"without a doubt, a firmly established fact; something that has definitely been accomplished."* God has placed this word here so that we would recognize this as something that is guaranteed for us.

The word *"griefs"* in these passages of Scripture comes from the Hebrew word *"kholee"* which means sickness. It is translated this way in Deut. 7:15, Deut. 28:61, 1 Kings 17:17, 2 Kings 1:2, 2 Kings 8:8 and other places. The word *"sorrows"* in the Hebrew is *"makob"* which actually means *pain* and is translated this way in Job 33:19 and Jer. 51:8. So actually Isaiah 53:4 should have been translated, *"He hath borne our sicknesses and carried our pains."* Robert Young in his *Young's Literal Translation* translates Isaiah 53:3-5 this way:

> *"He is despised, and left of men, A man of pains, and acquainted with **sickness**, And as one hiding the face from us, He is despised, and we esteemed him not. Surely our **sicknesses** he hath borne, And our **pains** -- he hath carried them, And we -- we have esteemed him plagued, Smitten of God, and afflicted. And he is pierced for our transgressions, Bruised for our iniquities, The chastisement of our peace [is] on him, **And by his bruise there is healing to us."**

However, the best commentary on the Bible is the Bible. Also all Old Testament Scripture should be interpreted in the light of the New Testament. This is how the writer of the gospel of Matthew interpreted Isaiah 53:4, 5:

> *"That it might be fulfilled which was spoken by Esaias the prophet, saying Himself took our infirmities, and bare our sicknesses."* (Matt. 8:17)

This proves beyond a shadow of a doubt that sickness and disease were covered in Christ's atonement. Jesus took upon Himself our sicknesses and diseases. He was our substitute. If He paid the bill then we need not pay it. He carried our sicknesses as though we had borne them ourselves. Therefore we need not accept something that Christ has already taken away.

Now I realize that the devil has given the opponents of healing in the atonement an answer to this. They will say that this Scripture states that this was fulfilled during the time of Jesus ministry. Therefore, according to them, this was fulfilled before the cross so sickness and disease is not covered in the atonement.

My only reply is this. If one part of Isaiah 53 can be interpreted that way then it should all be interpreted in this manner. This is including verse 10 where His soul was made an offering for sin. If that's true then "getting saved" or "getting born again" is impossible because without the shedding of blood there is no remission (Heb. 9:22). This argument against healing in the atonement is stupid in light of clear Scriptural teaching and plain common sense.

Besides that, Matthew is not the only New Testament writer who offers commentary on Isa. 53:

"Who his own self bare our sins in his own body on the tree, that we being dead to sins, should live unto righteousness: by whose stripes ye were healed." (1 Pet. 2:24)

Notice that there is a slight difference between Isaiah and Peter. Isaiah says that by His stripes we "are" healed. Peter tells us that by His stripes we "were" healed. Isaiah was giving the Old Testament saints something to look forward to. Peter tells us something that has been accomplished for us.

Healing has been made available to you by the death of Jesus upon the cross. Here is a truth that we must all learn to grasp: <u>God has already made healing available so He is not GOING to heal because He HAS healed.</u> What we must learn to do is appropriate that healing by faith. Faith believes that what God has made available to me is already mine even though I do not have it physically (Mark 11:22-24; Heb. 11:1; 2 Pet. 1:3, 4). As I exercise my faith to take what is rightfully mine then I will soon have its physical manifestation.

Jesus received these stripes when He was beaten on His back with a whip by Roman soldiers. I am told that these whips were plaited rope with drops of lead or sharp bones. When a muscle-bound Roman soldier would rare back and hit the body of a man with all his might with one of these whips this would tear the flesh. Of course massive bleeding would occur.

The Bible tells us that by His stripes we are healed. We know that atonement can only be made by blood, so therefore it is the blood of Jesus that deals with our sins and our sicknesses. Those who say that healing is not part of the atonement are actually saying that the blood of Jesus is not sufficient to deal with ALL of the results of sin. However, Peter shows us under the inspiration of the Spirit that the blood of Jesus has not only destroyed sin and sickness, but will continue to protect you from it.

Here is another practical truth for you to take hold of: <u>When sickness attacks your body or anyone in your home, Plead the blood over your body and over your home</u>. There is nothing that brings fear to Satan and his demons more than the mention of the blood of Jesus. It was this blood that defeated him in every area. In a later lesson we will prove to you from the Bible that Satan is the source of all sickness and disease.

Some years ago one Sunday I had preached a sermon on how the blood of Jesus overcomes the devil. Later that same week I became sick with a fever. I began complaining about my sickness (I was a real man of faith, wasn't I). The Lord reminded me of what I had preached on and told me to listen to the tape. I usually do not care to listen to my own sermon tapes.

Nevertheless I obeyed the Lord and I noticed some things I said about the blood of Jesus when I was under the anointing that I had forgotten. I began to plead the blood of Jesus over myself and commanded the devil to leave my body. I began to thank and praise God for His precious blood. A few minutes later the fever left and I was completely healed.

Jesus is the Passover lamb who was sacrificed for us (John 1:29, 36; 1 Cor. 5:7; 1 Pet. 1:18, 19; Rev. 5:6; 12:11). The lamb sacrificed in the Passover was a TYPE of Jesus and His atonement. Look at what the blood of the Passover lamb did for the Israelites as they applied its blood:

"And the blood shall be to you for a token upon the houses where ye are: and when I see the blood, I will pass over you, and the plague shall not come upon you to destroy, when I smite the land of Egypt." (Exodus 12:13)

A plague is a type of sickness and disease. The blood of a TYPE of Jesus was able to ward off this disease and protect God's people. If that is true of the TYPE, then it should be even more true of the real thing. Learn to plead the blood of Jesus and confess God's Word and you will be protected and healed of all sickness and disease.

I once preached a message on how the blood delivered us from sin and Satan. Not too long after that I was attacked with a fever. The Lord told me to listen to the tape of my sermon and learn to practice what I preach. I usually don't like to listen to my own tapes but I knew to obey God when He spoke. As I listened to the tape and heard the Holy Spirit speak through my voice I began to thank God for the blood of Jesus. I was instantly healed. The blood of Jesus has more than sufficient power to destroy sin, sickness, and all of the other works of the devil.

More New Testament proof that clearly shows that Jesus took our sicknesses and diseases on the cross can be found in Galatians 3:13:

"Christ hath redeemed us from the curse of the law, being made a curse for us: for it is written, cursed is everyone that hangeth on a tree."

Deuteronomy 28 tells us exactly what the curse of the law is. It lists all kinds of sicknesses and diseases, known and unknown. This was the curse for breaking the law. Christ took all of this upon Himself on the cross. There is no reason to receive any sickness or disease since Christ has redeemed us from it through His atonement for us.

Both First Peter and Galatians make reference to the cross of Christ as a tree. Once again as we search the Old Testament we find it's type therein:

> *"And he cried unto the Lord; and the Lord shewed him a TREE, which when he had cast into the waters, the waters were made sweet: there he made for them a statute and an ordinance, and there he proved them, And said, If thou wilt diligently hearken to the voice of the Lord thy God, and wilt do that which is right in His sight, and wilt give ear to his commandments, and keep all his statutes, I will put none of these diseases upon thee, which I have brought upon the Egyptians: for I am the LORD THAT HEALETH THEE."* (Ex. 15:25, 26)

Notice how the tree being thrown into the waters to make them sweet is connected to God's covenant name, Jehovah Rophe - The Lord that healeth thee. Jesus dying on the tree as our substitute proves the truth of that which Israel only possessed a type and shadow. You and I have the real thing. Our sicknesses were laid on that tree. Thank God we need not take them back.

Again notice that the scripture reads that *Moses* threw the tree into the bitter waters. God by divine revelation showed Moses the provision for the healing of the waters, yet, had he not *applied* the provision, the Israelites would have died of thirst. By divine revelation God has revealed the cross of Christ and the provision it has made for our healing. The reason many die from sickness and disease is because they do not apply the provision. Just as Moses applied the tree by faith, we must also by faith apply the tree that Christ died on by recognizing that our sicknesses and diseases were laid there. Just as Moses took the necessary actions by faith, we must also take the actions that are necessary to appropriate healing.

Let us examine one last bit of Scriptural evidence to prove the truth of our healing in the atonement. In Numbers 21 The children of Israel began speaking against God and Moses. This sin opened the door for fiery serpents to come and attack them.

This should be a lesson to all of us: Never speak against God or the man of God. This will open the door for Satan to attack you. These serpents were a type of Satan and his demons who come to inflict sickness and death upon the disobedient. If you are sick perhaps you should check this area. Have you spoken words against your pastor or some other servant of God? If so repent before God and your pastor and you will be healed.

However God in His mercy provided a means whereby the people could receive healing for the snake bites:

> *"And Moses made a serpent of brass, and put it upon a pole, and it came to pass, that if a serpent had bitten any man, when he beheld the serpent of brass, he lived."* (Num. 21:9)

This, as many of the other Old Testament types, was meant to convey a truth concerning Jesus:

> *"And as Moses lifted up the serpent in the wilderness, even so must the Son of man be lifted up."* (John 3:14)

As the sickness that was inflicted upon the people was healed after looking upon the brass serpent, so is the sickness that Satan and his demons bring are healed as we look to Christ. By putting a serpent on a pole, Moses demonstrated the victory that Jesus was to obtain over the devil upon the cross since Satan is also known as a serpent (Rev. 12:9).

As the people looked to the serpent of brass, a type of Christ, and received their healing, we also can look to the real thing and receive our healing as well as all of the other benefits of salvation.

A. B. Simpson, in his book, The Lord For The Body, offers some further insight:

> "The serpent seems to point to the lifting up of the Son of Man on the cross. And it seems almost as if Jesus took the serpent right into His arms and received his poison and his sting that we might

escape. Jesus took the serpent's sting and the serpent's poison into His own heart and into His own life, and, therefore, we may be free. Having borne in His body what our body deserves to bear, why should we bear it too? Why should you be stung by the devil's fangs when He was stung for you?" {2}

We can agree with Mr. Simpson's interpretation because 1 Corinthians 10:9-10 proves beyond a shadow of a doubt that the destroyer was responsible for bringing the serpents in to the camp of Israel. Satan is the one who comes to steal, kill, and destroy and therefore that makes him the destroyer (John 10:10). However, we must remember that the Israelites opened the door to Satan by murmuring and complaining (Num. 11:1).

Many will interpret this passage as Jesus only giving eternal life to those who look to Him. However, if healing is not provided in this salvation then Israel had something better than we did with just a "type" of the real thing. They had both salvation and health.

The word salvation in the Greek is *SOZO*. According to Strong's Concordance it means, " *To save, deliver or protect, heal, preserve, so well, be whole.* "{3} This word is the word used in Matt. 14:35-36, Mark 5:34, Acts 4:9 and other passages of Scripture when dealing with the healing of the sick. It is the same word used in Romans 10:9-10 -- the Scripture we give to sinners to show them how to receive salvation.

So we see that salvation is not only forgiveness of sins and a free ticket to heaven when we die. Healing and deliverance comes with the package too. Do not let the lies of man and Satan deceive you in only taking part of the package. Appropriate ALL that Christ has made available by His death upon the cross.

The problem is that too many people have spent more time trying to give reasons why God does not bestow upon His children such wonderful blessings anymore. If our scholars and theologians would spend more time accepting the TRUTH instead of trying to prove a lie then we would have stronger and healthier warriors in the body of Christ.

We have shown you much Scripture to prove to you this truth of healing in the atonement. It was necessary to do so because Satan has attacked this truth concerning healing more than any other. When people are in doubt as to whether healing was part of the redemption price, they will not have faith to receive. Satan knows this and has therefore done a thorough job of deceiving good Christians in this area. We find it necessary to do a thorough job in making this truth clear to as many as will receive it.

Healing is part of your salvation. You can receive this just as you have received the assurance that you will go to heaven when you die. Christ paid a heavy price so that you can have divine health. Receive this blessing in Jesus name.

Chapter Four

Sickness Is The Result Of Sin, Therefore Healing Must Accompany Forgiveness

"So God's blessings are given to us by faith, as a free gift; WE ARE CERTAIN TO GET THEM....." (Rom. 4:16; Living Bible)

In these lessons we are giving you seven indisputable truths concerning divine healing. We want you to know beyond a shadow of a doubt that divine healing is yours and is guaranteed to you.

We have seen that it is God's will to heal, it is His desire to heal, and that Jesus bore all sicknesses and disease as well as sin in His substitutionary death. In this lesson we want to show you that sickness has its origin in sin.

If sickness has its origin in sin then we should be able to appropriate healing as well as forgiveness. Ninety eight percent of all Christians have no problems believing that God forgives sin. Nevertheless many of these same people have a struggle believing that it is just as much a part of God's plan to deliver us from the results of our sin.

The reason behind this is because many of these people have been deceived. They either believe that sickness is a blessing used to mature them or they believe that it is just a natural part of living. They believe that since they are in the world they must accept these things.

We should also realize that living holy will protect us from sickness. We are told, *"For sin shall not have dominion over you."* (Rom. 6:14). If sickness has its origin in sin and if we are able to walk in dominion over sin then we should also be able to walk in dominion over sickness.

When you see that sickness and sin go hand in hand you will also see that neither should be tolerated. We should learn to receive

---

our healing of sickness as well as our forgiveness of sin. As we resist the temptation to sin, we should also resist the temptation to get sick.

When God spoke to Adam concerning fruit that should not be eaten He said this:

"But of the tree of the knowledge of good and evil, thou shalt not eat of it: for in the day that thou eatest thereof thou shalt surely die." (Gen. 2:17)

This was a direct commandment from God almighty. God meant for this command to be obeyed. This was God's law to Adam. Any transgression of God's law is sin (1 John 3:4).

Adam was given dominion over the whole earth (Gen. 1:26-31), and as long as Adam allowed Jehovah to be His ruler then Jehovah God would be ruling the earth through Adam. Righteousness and holiness would reign upon the earth as a result of Adam's yielding to Jehovah's lordship. God would keep the earth free of anything that could hurt or harm because the ruler of the earth was submissive to Him.

However, by transgressing God's law, Adam submitted himself to another ruler. Whoever sins is of the devil, the originator and inventor of sin (John 8:44; 1 John 3:8). Adam was given full charge and responsibility of the earth. By submitting himself to Satan and allowing Satan to be his lord, Adam gave the earth over to sin and unrighteousness. As a result, death reigned upon the earth:

"Wherefore, as by one man sin entered into the world, and death by sin; and so death passed upon all men, for that all have sinned." (Rom. 5:12)

Notice that it was by one MAN that sinned entered into the world. Satan could not bring his unholy reign into the world because he was not left in charge of it. However, when he found someone who would submit to him then he was able to bring his program in to replace the program of holiness and righteousness.

As a result of sin death came. It came first spiritually. Man was separated from God. As with all spiritual things, it soon manifested itself into the physical realm. Death had to find a way to manifest itself and so sickness and disease were its weapon.

The Bible leaves us with no doubt that sickness is the result of sin, or a transgression of God's holy law:

> *"Be careful to obey everything in these teachings. They are written in this book. You must respect the glorious and wonderful name of the Lord your God. The Lord will give you terrible diseases to you and to your descendants. You will have long and serious diseases. You will have long and miserable sicknesses. And the Lord will give you all the diseases of Egypt that you dread. And the diseases will stay with you. The Lord will also give you every disease and sickness not written in this book"* (Deut. 28:58-61; The Everyday Bible).

Now understand that when God says that "He" will give them sicknesses and diseases it is not making him the source or origin of the sickness. He has established the law of sowing and reaping. Whatever a man sows is that which he reaps. When a man sows to his flesh he will reap corruption in the flesh (Gal. 6:7, 8).

God is the only person qualified to decide what is right and wrong. That makes Him the perfect judge. As the judge He must be fair in His judgment. If someone does something worthy of death then judgment is passed upon that person. Though God is the judge, this does not mean that He always takes an active role in executing the judgment. We will see in a later lesson that Satan is the primary agent responsible for placing sickness and disease upon man. However, God has established the law of sowing and reaping and remains bound to His Word, even if it is not His perfect will that any be sick and placed under Satan's bondage.

When Paul was teaching the Corinthians the proper way of taking the Lord's supper, he made every effort to discourage the abuses of it that were taking place among them at that time. He told them that their abuses was the reason for their sicknesses and premature deaths

"For this cause many are weak and sickly among you, and many sleep. For if we judge ourselves, we should not be judged. But when we are JUDGED, we are chastened of the Lord, that we should not be condemned with the world." (1 Cor. 11:30-32)

We see in the case of the Corinthians that God was judging them. Due to His holiness, God is left with no other choice but to judge sin. Rather than taking an active role in carrying out a sentence, a judge often places this duty in the hands of the prison wardens or executioners (1 Cor. 5:1-5; 1 Tim. 1:20: Ps. 78:49; Matt 18:34-35). <u>Now here's the key: if we judge ourselves there will never be any need for God to judge us. He has given us His Word and has shown us right from wrong.</u>

When we sin we can run to the Lord right away and receive forgiveness. As we are washed from our sins by the blood then we are made to reap the corruption that we have sown to our flesh. We can abort the seed of corruption this way. As we are tempted then we can judge ourselves so that we do not yield to temptation which when conceived would bring forth death (James 1:13-16).

Some may not agree with me but we must all agree with this: sickness is the result of disobedience to God's law. Satan, not God, is the one who moves people to disobey God. Whether we choose to believe that God is the proprietor of sickness or we choose to believe that Satan is, we must remember that Satan moves people to sin. Sin puts us in a position to get sick, therefore Satan is still the one who is ultimately responsible.

Jesus also taught that sickness was the result of sin. After healing a man at the pool of Bethesda he gave him a warning:

"Afterward Jesus findeth him in the temple, and said unto him, Behold, thou art whole: sin no more lest a worse thing come unto thee." (John 5:14)

Obviously this man's sin opened the door for sickness to come in his life. If this were not true then Jesus would not have told him to sin no more. Notice that Jesus did not say, "sin no more unless God put a worse thing on you." No. We are taught from this example that we are personally responsible for what happens to us concerning sickness and disease. This man could sin and get sick again or he could endeavour to live holy and stay in good health.

We can see from Scripture that sickness is the direct result of sin, but we also see that we can have victory over both. Both are the works of the devil. Jesus by His death, burial, and resurrection has obtained for us victory over all of the works of our enemy.

When God revealed one of His covenant names to Israel, He told them how they could continually walk in the benefits of that covenant:

".....If thou wilt diligently hearken to the voice of the Lord thy God, and wilt do that which is right in his sight, and wilt give ear to his commandments, and keep all his statutes, I will put none of these diseases upon thee, which I have brought upon the Egyptians: for I am the Lord that healeth thee." (Ex. 15:26)

In order for Israel to appropriate this covenant blessing of healing they were to walk in obedience to God. They had to live free of sin. His covenant name is "the Lord that healeth thee" and not "the Lord that maketh thee sick if you mess up." However, when there is sin in a person's life they are walking from under the umbrella of covenant protection and leave themselves open to attacks from the devil.

Proverbs also teaches this principle:

"Be not wise in thine own eyes: fear the Lord, and depart from evil. It shall be health to thy navel, and marrow to thy bones." (Proverbs 3:7, 8)

A departure from evil is a guarantee of divine health. This is a wonderful promise. As we live free from evil we are guaranteed to live free of its results.

John shows us that the divine health and prosperity that God offers will come in proportion to how we allow our spirits to prosper:

"Beloved, I wish above all things that thou mayest prosper and be in health, EVEN AS thy soul prospereth." (3 John 2)

Notice that this wish for Gaius which was inspired by the Holy Spirit and meant for our appropriation could only come "even as" his soul prospered. When we feed upon God's word and we do not allow our spirits to be tainted with sin then our souls will prosper. However, when we live a life of sin we close the doors to God's blessings of health and prosperity, even though it is His wish to give them to us.

The Good news is that once we have repented and received forgiveness of our sins we become eligible to receive healing for our bodies. When Jesus was in a house preaching, some men ripped off the roof of this house and lowered a paralyzed man down to receive his healing. Jesus knew the that the man came seeking HEALING, however He first dealt with the core of his sickness:

"When Jesus saw their faith, he said unto the sick of the palsy, Son, thy sins be forgiven thee." (Mark 2:5)

Now Jesus knew how to analyze the problem correctly. There are people today who are sick but will not repent of sin in their life. Yet they are still waiting for God to heal them. God, in His love is continually trying to move them towards repentance so that He will be able to heal them. God wants us to deal with the actual problem and then He can deal with the symptoms.

Then there are others, who like this man, may be living in a state of condemnation. The devil is constantly beating them down with condemnation and unworthiness. Though they want to receive forgiveness and healing they do not have the faith because the devil is constantly bringing their sins before

their face and telling them that God is mad at them and does not want to forgive or heal them.

Jesus knew this and before He could get the man healed He first had to build His faith. He had to know that whatever sins caused him to fall into that condition were forgiven. The religious leaders did not like that. They tolerated Jesus' healing ministry but his ministering forgiveness was something else. However, Jesus said this:

"For whether is easier to say, Thy sins be forgiven thee; or to say, Arise and walk? But that ye may know that the Son of man hath power on earth to forgive sins, (then saith he to the sick of the palsy,) Arise, take up thy bed and go unto thine house. And he arose, and departed unto his house." (Matt. 9:5-7)

Back then the religious leaders tolerated healing of the sick but opposed any forgiving of sins. Today, many religious leaders believe in the forgiveness of sins but oppose the healing of the sick. Satan has reversed the trend of controversy to fit the times.

Nevertheless Jesus shows that forgiving of sins and healing are by the same authority. It takes faith to appropriate both. Many times one has to have an assurance that his or her sins are forgiven before they can receive the healing of their body.

The Bible couples the forgiveness of sin with healing:

"Bless the Lord, O my soul, and forget not his benefits: Who forgiveth ALL thine iniquities; who healeth ALL thy diseases" (Ps. 103:2, 3)

If healing was not the will of God and if He did not want you to have it He would not have commanded us to "forget not" His benefits. Notice that He does not forgive SOME sins and not forgive others. Some people think that their sins are too big to receive forgiveness. Others think that they have sinned or committed a particular sin too often to receive mercy. Jesus died and took ALL of your sin upon Himself. You can constantly appropriate forgiveness.

Just the same, God heals ALL of your diseases. There is no disease that God cannot heal. He specializes in those impossible cases; the ones beyond medical treatment. Most of all we see from this passage that God's benefits include both forgiveness AND healing. If one is for the church today then both are for the church today.

In the New Testament we can see that both forgiveness and healing are for the church:

> *"And the prayer of faith shall save the sick, and the Lord shall raise him up; and if he have committed sins, they shall be forgiven him. Confess your faults one to another, that ye may be healed."* (James 5:15, 16)

Some years ago one of our neighbors who was also a Christian came to our house. When she came in my wife and I could see that she was in much pain. She asked, "Troy and Takako, could you please pray for my back. It's hurting very badly."

I had her read this Scripture and then I asked her, "Do you believe this?" She told me that she did. I then instructed her to pray according to this Scripture and confess any known sin to God. My wife and I laid hands on her and she began to pray while we rebuked the pain on her back. She was immediately healed.

She told me afterwards that she had been angry with her husband concerning some things he had done when the pain came on her. When I had given her James 5:14-15 she knew that she had to first confess her sins before she could be healed. When she did that she felt the healing power of God come on her. We all rejoiced together, thanking and praising God for His promises.

Sickness has its origin with sin. Jesus died that we might be free from both.

We are not implying that every person who is sick are suffering as the result of some *personal* sin in their life. We realize that there have been some wonderful saints of God who have been mightily used of Him. However, these same wonderful Christians are either on a sick bed right now or have gone on to be with the Lord. When Jesus' disciples inquired about whether a certain blind had sinned or if his parents had sinned and caused this man's condition, Jesus answered them "neither" (John 9:1-3).

We are saying that if there was never any sin in the world, sickness would not be here either. Sickness is the direct result of sin whether the sick person sinned personally or not. The germs and disease came when Satan became ruler of this world.

We are merely teaching that if Christians have the opportunity to appropriate the best that God has for them. Unfortunately many dear saints who have excelled in many spiritual areas are ignorant of this truth or refuse to believe it. Yet it is available to all of God's children. Sin and sickness go hand in hand, so does forgiveness and healing.

Chapter Five

Satan: The Primary Source Of Sickness

We are proving from the Bible that healing is yours, it belongs to you and you should have it. The best proof of this is not theology, scholarly academic study, or even experience. The best proof is facts based on what the Bible says about it.

If you believe the Bible literally then what we are teaching here should build your faith and you should recognize that healing is yours. If you believe what most men have said about the Bible coupled with theology and dispensationalism then more than likely you will not receive these truths. Do you truly desire to receive the healing that is rightfully yours as a child of God? Then you must close your mind to all opposing views and simply accept God's Word for what it plainly teaches.

We do not teach these truths to try to convince those who oppose healing. We already know that they refuse to believe no matter how much Scripture you show them. They already have an answer and an argument for everything. We write these things to help those who really want to know the truth and are willing to accept it.

It should be no wonder to us that Satan has deceived so many ministers concerning healing. They believe that it is either not for today or that it is not God's will to heal everyone. Many of these individuals are good men and women who love the Lord Jesus, yet refuse to accept this truth that is so vital to the gospel.

In our first lesson we showed you three views held in the Body of Christ concerning God's will toward healing. In this lesson allow me to show you four views held in the church regarding God's attitude toward sickness:

A. God puts sickness on people to punish them for sins and misbehavior.

B. God puts sickness on His children to try, test, and humble them. This turns out to be a "blessing in disguise."

C. God may not be the author of sickness but He ALLOWS the sickness in the life of the believer for the two reasons stated above.

D. Satan is the author of sickness. God hates anything of satanic origin and has sent His Son to die that we may be free of it. God does not expect the believer to tolerate anything that originates with the devil.

I strongly advocate the fourth view (view D). The first view (view A) has some scriptural merit and should not be dismissed outright by those of us who teach the truth concerning divine healing. There is scriptural support for it in both the Old and New Testaments.{1} Nonetheless, too many theologians and religionists have over-emphasized view A and have totally neglected view D.

These all too happy advocates of view A have also taught this view as though God received some perverted pleasure from bringing discipline from sickness when such was necessary. Therefore, these lessons will put the primary focus on view D. We will demonstrate to the reader that Satan, and not God, desires your sickness while God desires our freedom from sin and sickness.

In our last lesson we showed you that although God is the judge, and often pronounces the punishment that corresponds with sin, He does not will or desire the sickness of His people anymore than He desires or wills any sinner to go to hell (Ezek. 18:32; Luke 7:30; 1 Tim. 2:4; 2 Pet. 3:9.) Therefore, the second view (view B) is to be rejected outright by the Bible believing Christian.

The third view has some element of truth to it but it is not totally true. It is to be hoped that you will understand what we mean by this as you study this lesson.

In Genesis we see the creation of man's body:

"And the Lord formed man of the DUST of the ground....." (Gen. 2:7)

Keep in mind that man's body was formed from the dust of the ground. God makes reference to this fact after Adam has sinned and sold his dominion over the earth to the devil:

".....for dust THOU ART, and unto dust shalt thou return." (Gen. 3:19)

God reminds Adam that he is dust. This is what his body was used to form his body. Others in the Bible came to this same conclusion (Gen. 18:27; Job 34:15; Ps. 103:14; Eccl. 3:20). So we can see that dust is symbolic of man's body.

As the dust is symbolic of the body of man, the serpent is symbolic of Satan (Rev. 12:9; Luke 10:18, 19). Notice the curse pronounced upon the serpent:

".....upon thy belly shalt thou go, and DUST SHALT THOU EAT all the days of thy life." (Gen. 3:14)

This was a literal curse upon the serpent but there is also a deeper spiritual truth. Since the serpent is symbolic of the devil and dust is symbolic of man's body then the devil was given rights to feed upon man's body.

These rights were not given by God. We must remember that man was given dominion over all the earth. He was God's under ruler. Nevertheless, God warned him that disobedience to His commands would result in death (Gen. 2:17). Having this knowledge, the man disobeyed anyway. Therefore man gave Satan rights to his body and the body of those who would come from his loins. God was simply pronouncing the judgment and curse that man brought upon himself and his descendants.

God, in pronouncing the curse acted in His role as JUDGE since He was the one who established the laws as creator and king of all the universe. However God did not pronounce His sentence upon ignorant creatures. Adam and the devil both knew what they were doing when they did it.

My friend, we cannot place the blame on God. Adam had dominion and could have stopped him. With authority comes responsibility. Adam had the responsibility of preventing the devil from taking that which God had given to man. Instead, Adam followed his wife in rebellion and got in league with the devil. Satan became his master and was given rights to his body. God cannot be blamed for this. God did not punish him. Adam placed himself under the curse. God out of love warned him and he disobeyed. God so loved that in spite of this disobedience He promised a savior to deliver man from the results of his own sin (Gen. 3:15).

When man turned the authority of this world over to the devil, evil began to reign in this world. Satan is by nature evil. Several places in the Bible he is referred to as the evil one (1 Thess. 3:3; Matt. 5:37; 6:13; John 17:15; 1 John 2:14). The demonic forces that work for him and who are the source of much sickness and disease are also called evil (Luke 7:21; 8:2; Acts 19:12-16). God has given us His description of sickness and disease:

*"And the LORD will take away from thee all sickness, and will put none of the **evil diseases** of Egypt, which thou knowest, upon thee; but will lay them upon all them that hate thee."* (Deut. 7:15)

The Bible tells us that Satan and his spiritual forces are evil. God also says that sickness and disease is evil. It stands to reason that Satan wills and desires our sickness and disease while God wills and desires our healing and health. God is Good (Ps. 34:8; 106:1; 107:1), does not tempt us with evil (James 1:13;NIV), does not do evil (Job 34:10;NIV), and takes no pleasure in it. Evil is NEVER in the will of God for His creatures. In contrast, nothing that is good will find it's origin in Satan. Sickness and disease are evil and the evil one is its primary source.

Now someone may ask, "It says at the latter part of that verse that God will lay them upon all that hate thee. Doesn't that make Him the source?" NO! Look at the word "lay" in this passage. It comes from the Hebrew word "nathan."{2} This word same word is used in Exodus 12:23:

*"For the Lord will pass through to smite the Egyptians; and when he seeth the blood upon the lintel, and on the two side posts, the Lord will pass over the door, and will not **SUFFER** THE DESTROYER to come in unto your houses to smite you."* (Ex. 12:23)

The word *"suffer"* comes from the same Hebrew word used in Deuteronomy 7:15 that is translated *"lay."* The Amplified Bible translates the latter part of verse 23 this way: *".....the Lord will pass over the door and will not ALLOW the destroyer to come into your houses to slay you."* While there is some dispute between commentators and other Bible students concerning the identity of the "destroyer" in the above passage, I have no doubt that this is a reference to Satan. The following comments written over 100 years ago in a Christian magazine may prove interesting to the reader:

In Exodus xii. 23 we see how God and the destroyer work. The latter is permitted to select a single victim from each family, and is restrained in all else. Hence the work is said to be God's, though in reality the good only is his, and the evil Satan's. God says, " I will smite," but immediately refers to the real agent, and says, " I will not suffer The Destroyer to come into your houses to smite you." Thus when one inspired writer tells us that God blinds the minds of men, another that Satan does so, and a third that man does so, we perceive that all these statements are correct—the act being done by the permission of the first, the agency of the second, and the wilful sin of the third; in other words God quiescent, Satan active, man willing.

When therefore we read that God hardened Pharaoh's heart, we understand that Pharaoh's state of unbelief had driven far from him that Spirit of Truth that hateth iniquity, and cannot dwell with evil, whereon error worked uncontrolled in Pharaoh. When Truth is remote or quiescent, error is present and dominant. If the protecting shield of the one be withdrawn, the sword of the other must fall.

Similarly God says, "I will bring evil on this people, the fruit of their thoughts" (Jer. vi. 19). And while He is repeatedly said to have destroyed Israel, it is added for our learning, "O Israel ! thou hast destroyed thyself." God is expressly termed "Israel's Help "(Hosea xiii. 9); in no sense, therefore, is He the destroyer, that is the title of the great god of this world.{3}

The above comments confirm for us how God is often credited with doing those things in which He only permitted. I would agree with the writer that God Himself is NOT the destroyer. As discipline for the fornicator in the Corinthian church, Paul instructed them *"To deliver such a one as this, unto **Satan, for the destruction of the flesh** ...."* (1 Cor. 5:5).

The sincere student of Scripture must understand that the translators of the Old Testament often understood the Hebrew language to make God the cause of something that He only permitted. Joseph Rotherham, stated that in his excellent Bible translation "....he has endeavoured to avoid representing God as the author or instigator of wickedness". He further states that:

> That Hebrew Grammars distinctly avow occasion or permission to be sometimes the sense of verbs which ordinarily signify cause can be verified by a reference to the Hebrew Grammar of Gesenius, say in the admirable translation of Dr. Benjamin Davies (p. 120). After stating that the verbal form (conjugation) called piel denotes intensity and repetition, this grammar adds: "It often takes the modifications expressed by permit, to declare or hold as, to help.{4}

Based on the Corinthians passage, we see that Satan is the "destroyer" while God permits him to do this destruction to those who have left rebelled against Him through unrepentant sin as Pharaoh did. This should also help us to see Deuteronomy 7:15 in a new light. Based on the Hebrew grammatical insight from Rotherham, it is possible that the Hebrew word "Nathan" translated in this passage could be used in a permissive sense as it is being used in Exodus 12:23. So an alternative understanding is that God would *allow* Satan to put sickness upon all the ones that hated His covenant people. In other words, He would not protect Israel's enemies from Satan's onslaughts.{5}

Nevertheless, as we will see later, losing God's protection from Satanic oppression is by *choice* and not by God's *design*. By becoming enemies of God's people, Israel's enemies were becoming enemies of God which placed them in Satan's territory and removed any right to receive protection from God.

However, you are a BLOOD BOUGHT CHILD OF GOD. Just as God saw the blood on the lintel and on the door of every Israelites house, He sees the blood of Jesus upon you. When Satan tries to attack you with sickness remind him that you have the blood upon you and that he is NOT ALLOWED to come in to you or your home with it. The blood protects YOU from sickness and disease as it did the Israelites.

Job is another case proving Satan, not God, is the author of sickness. The Bible makes it very clear who put sickness upon Job:

"So went Satan from the presence of the Lord, and smote Job with sore boils from the sole of his foot unto his crown." (Job 2:7)

So many churches seem to teach the book of Job in a way that makes god the agent of Job's tragedies. Satan is given either no mention or is made to have a very minor role. Others who acknowledge the devil's role seem to believe that God manipulated him into doing what was done to Job.

Job was a very wonderful man who loved God. Satan also knew this and targeted Job for destruction as he does to every child of God (1 Pet. 5:8-10). Satan attempted his destruction of Job by first accusing Job of serving God for only what Job could get out of it and also accusing God of only blessing Job to win his loyalty and devotion. Satan challenged God by to see what Job would do if all of the blessings he were given were taken from him. Job was simply the unfortunate victim of a war between God and the devil.

Nevertheless, we cannot accept Satan's attacks on Job and how Job dealt with them as a pattern for us today. Job did not have a Bible as we have so he knew nothing about a devil who hated him. You and I do not have that excuse today. We have been given full knowledge of who the devil is and how to resist him and stand against his tactics (Mark 16:15-20; Luke 10:17-20; Eph. 4:27; 6:10-18; James 4:7)

It is also possible that Job could have opened the door for Satan's attacks through fear (Job 1:4, 5). He lived fearing the negative (Job 3:25). As the well known Bible Commentator, Matthew Henry wrote, "Even in his former prosperous state troubles were continually feared; so that then he was never easy, Job_3:25, Job_3:26 ... He was afraid for his children when they were feasting, lest they should offend God (Job_1:5), afraid for his servants lest they should offend his neighbours"{6}

While we should avoid dogmatism concerning this, the possibility that Job may have been living in fear could cause the hedge of protection around him to be broken (Job 1:9-12; Eccl. 10:8). Regardless of whether or not this is true, we must remember that it was Satanic activity, and not God, that is at fault for Job's tragedies. On the other hand, when Job repented for his actions and prayed for his friends he was completely healed:

> *"And the Lord turned the captivity of Job....."* (Job 42:10)

God's divine commentary of Job's situation was not that it was a blessing. God called it CAPTIVITY. However, God was powerful enough to turn it. God does not want His people being taken CAPTIVE by sickness, disease, poverty, sin or any other work of the devil. The good news that we find in Job 42 is that no matter what Satan brings our way, God can TURN IT. We do not have to live with the attacks of the devil. We can pray just as Job did and expect God to heal and deliver.

Jesus proves this truth to us in the New Testament. A woman who had a spirit of infirmity for 18 years came to our Lord and received healing. Unfortunately it was another one of those Sabbath day healings that was making Jesus quite unpopular with the religious people. However, Jesus said:

> *"And ought not this woman, being a daughter of Abraham, whom Satan hath BOUND, lo, these eighteen years, be loosed from this bond on the Sabbath day?"* (Luke 18:16)

He called this woman's sickness bondage. He called Job's sickness captivity. We see that Satan is responsible for the captivity and bondage that is placed on men and woman today through sickness and disease. This is God's attitude towards sickness. It is not a blessing that will mature you and teach you. God has His word and His ministry gifts for that purpose (Eph. 4:11-13).

So far we see that the Scriptures tell us that Satan is behind sickness and disease. Since that is true allow me to offer a basic definition for divine healing. Divine healing is simply God restoring the body back to the condition (or a better condition) that it was before the attack that Satan brought upon it.

God says that sickness is evil, captivity, and bondage as is all of the other works of the devil. God is not going around putting sickness on people and neither is He ALLOWING Satan to do it. He has sent Jesus to deliver us from this evil work of Satan:

"How God anointed Jesus of Nazareth with the Holy Ghost and with power: who went about doing good, and healing all that were oppressed of the devil; for God was with him." (Acts 10:38)

The word *"oppress"* in the Greek means to *"exercise power over"* (Vines){4}. Webster's Dictionary says that it is *"to crush or burden by abuse of power or authority."*{7} Satan was given rights over man's body in the garden. As any dictator who gets into power he began to exercise those rights by oppressing man. Sickness is meant to crush you and destroy you under Satan's power. It is meant to keep you captive and in bondage so that you cannot serve God in the best manner possible.

The Bible tells us that Jesus went about doing GOOD. Notice the contrast between the works of Jesus and the works of the devil. Jesus HEALED. The divine commentary on that is that this healing was "good." The devil OPPRESSED. There is nothing good about that. The devil's work of sickness and disease gets no acknowledgment of good from God. What men are calling a "blessing," God is calling it evil, captivity, bondage, oppression, death, and a curse. Whose commentary will you accept, God's or men?

When Jesus died on the cross and took the punishment for our sins, our bodies were released from the authority of Satan. He no longer has the right to exercise any authority over our bodies because they now belong to the Lord (1 Cor. 6:17-20). The only way that Satan can bring his works to you is if you let him. Jesus has destroyed the works of the devil:

> *"He that committeth sin is of the devil: for the devil sinneth from the beginning. For this purpose the Son of God was manifested, that he might destroy the works of the devil."* (1 John 3:8)

Anyone who sins submit themselves to the authority of the devil who is the author of all sin. We showed you in our last lesson that sickness is the result of sin. Satan has rights over the bodies of men and women because of sin, not because God allows him to or wills it.

Jesus destroyed the works of the devil. The word *"destroy"* in the Greek means *"to loose, dissolve, sever, break, demolish."* (Vines). If Jesus did all of this then we need not receive any sickness or disease. If sickness is attacking your body then take this Scripture and remind Satan that his works have been destroyed by Jesus. By faith praise the Lord for having destroyed the works of Satan in your body over 2000 years ago. In order for this to work you must be convinced beyond reason that sickness and disease are the works of the devil.

Let us look at the contrast again. When the Bible refers to any "work" that Jesus did it usually referred to healings, miracles, or getting people set free from any bondage or oppression (John 9:3-5; 10:32, 37, 38; 14:10-12). Never once have you read where Jesus put sickness and disease on people. Never once have you read that God called sickness "good" or a "blessing." God by nature is holy and good and therefore cannot do unto man that which is out of harmony with His nature.

Remember that Adam brought in the penalty for disobedience. That penalty was death. In Deuteronomy 28 God lists a number of blessings in the first 15 verses of this chapter. In the following verses He lists a bunch of curses for disobedience. These curses as we have seen in previous lessons mention many, many different types of sicknesses and diseases. In Deuteronomy 30 God gives another description of the blessings and curses:

> *"I call heaven and earth to record this day against you, that I have set before you LIFE AND DEATH, blessing and cursing: therefore CHOOSE LIFE that both thou and thy seed may live."* (Deut. 30:19)

The description God gives of the sicknesses and diseases listed in Deuteronomy 28 is DEATH. Nevertheless, He also makes it plain and clear that death is neither His will nor His desire for you. He exhorts us to choose LIFE, or in other words, choose the blessings He has made available.

Man has the choice. God does not allow sickness and disease to come as a result of His "sovereign will" as some would have us to believe. We believe in God's sovereignty but we also know that due to His sovereignty He has given man the choice. We have the ability to choose life or death. We have the choice to choose sickness and disease. In choosing the sickness or disease, God does not give you the sickness. Satan was the one who wielded the power of death:

> *"....that through death he (Jesus) might destroy him that had the power of death, that is the devil."* (Heb. 2:14)

God described the curses in Deuteronomy 28 as death. Satan had this power to exercise over the disobedient. Yet again the Scriptures give us the good news. Jesus DESTROYED the devil. Those who are submitted to Jesus need not put up with anything this defeated enemy dishes out to us. Look at what the next verse says:

> *"And DELIVER THEM who through fear of death were all their lifetime subject to bondage."* (Heb. 2:15)

Remember that sickness is captivity, bondage, and oppression. Jesus has delivered you from that. You no longer need to fear it but you can stand against it with bold faith armed with the covenant promises of God. Some people have fear because there may be a history of cancer in their family. Jesus has delivered you from that fear. We need not fear any heretical family sicknesses because the curse ceased when we made Jesus Christ our Lord (Gal. 3:13).

The word "destroy" in Hebrews 2:14 is a different Greek word then the one in 1 John 3:8. This word means to "abolish." It means to render inactive. Satan's activities of sickness have been rendered inactive in your body now that you belong to God. The choice you must make is to accept this as truth or to continue under what God calls bondage and oppression. Jesus came to deliver you from every work of the devil.

One last thing I want to deal with. Some question this type of teaching because of scientific proof that sickness comes from germs. If this is true then they say we cannot blame the devil for it. Dr. Paul (David) Yonggi Cho, Pastor of the largest church in the world based in South Korea says this:

> "Some people may ask: Diseases are from germs, aren't they? How can we say that disease is from the spirit of the devil? Here is an easy example: The life of man came into being when the seeds of life from his parents came together. Now, where does that life come from? It is from God himself. When God takes their life away, all human bodies are immediately subject to decay. The one who provides the life of destruction continually to all kinds of germs, which are the seeds of sickness, is none other than the devil. The primary function of sickness is to destroy the body. Sickness is brought by sin. And the devil, who is the incarnation of sin, takes control of the power of death." (From "Suffering... Why Me?"){8}

I believe that Dr. Cho offers an excellent explanation for this mystery. Even if you do not agree with Dr. Cho, we have given you enough Scripture to prove beyond a shadow of a doubt that it is Satan, not God, who feeds sickness to the body. Accept what God says and not man. Refuse reason and receive healing and health.

Chapter Six

Healing: Your Covenant Right

We are teaching you seven indisputable truths concerning divine healing that will impart and strengthen your faith. After studying these truths you should have no problems receiving divine healing.

So far we have shown you that it is God's will (His purpose) and His Desire (He wants to do it) to heal you. We have shown you that healing was provided in Christ's atoning death on the cross as well as forgiveness of sins and eternal life. We have shown you that sin and Satan are the sources of sickness. Anything that comes from these two sources need not and should not be tolerated.

In this lesson we want to show you from Scripture that healing is your covenant right. It is not merely a privilege of the blessed few. It is not just a matter of God's sovereign grace. It is actually your right according to the covenant that was established as the result of the shed blood of Jesus.

In Deuteronomy we see that healing was provided along with other blessings in the covenant that God established with Abraham, Isaac, and Jacob:

> *"Wherefore it shall come to pass, if ye hearken to these judgements, and keep, and do them, that the Lord thy God shall keep unto thee the COVENANT and the mercy which he sware **unto thy fathers**...... And the Lord will take away from thee ALL SICKNESS, and will put none of the evil diseases of Egypt, which thou knowest, upon thee; but will lay them upon all them that hate thee."* (Deut 7:12, 15).

Divine healing was included in the covenant that God made, not just with Israel, but with their fathers. Abraham was the first that

God made the covenant with. The covenant was reconfirmed through Isaac and Jacob. The New Testament clearly confirms that we are still a part of this covenant:

> *"Now to Abraham and his seed were the promises made. He saith not, And to seeds, as of many; but as of one, And to thy seed, which is Christ. And this I say, that the covenant, that was confirmed before of God in Christ, the law, which was four hundred years after, cannot disannul, that it should make the promise of none effect."* (Gal. 3:16, 17).

This chapter goes on to say:

> *"And if ye be Christ's, then are ye Abraham's seed, and heirs according to the promise."* (Gal. 3:29)

The Living Bible paraphrases this verse: *"And now that we are Christ's we are the true descendants of Abraham, and all of God's promises belong to us."* The word "belong" implies ownership. If something belongs to me then I have a RIGHT to it. If healing is part of the covenant then it is mine by right and it belongs to me.

This is the picture that we want you to understand. God made a covenant with the God of the fathers of Israel. Whenever the term "fathers" is used in this context it is speaking of Abraham, Isaac, and Jacob (Ex. 3:13-16; 4:5). Now you are the seed of Abraham through Jesus Christ. Every promise that God gave in His covenant to Abraham is yours also and it could not be disannulled because of the law that was established with Israel. Therefore, the promise of divine healing is just as much a covenant right for those who have made Jesus Christ their Lord and Savior as it was for Israel.

My friend, divine healing is a covenant promise that belongs to you as a seed of Abraham. Webster's dictionary tells us that a promise is *"a declaration that one will do or refrain from doing something specified; a legally binding declaration that gives the person to whom it is made a RIGHT to expect or claim the performance or forbearance of a specified act."* {1}

Many religious people have trouble believing that God has given His children certain rights and privileges, especially when it pertains to divine healing. Some years ago I was attending a church where some of the ministers were preaching against the so called "faith message." They were criticizing the teachings of men whom I personally believe to be men of God. One of the ministers, while commenting on God's blessings and benefits made this statement: "They are not called RIGHTS, they are PRIVILEGES."

Allow me to illustrate how the terms "rights and privileges" are used in modern vernacular. Then you will understand what people are saying when they tell you that God's blessings are only *privileges* and not something you have a *right* to. When I was in the Air Force I worked for an Air Force Career advisor. He counseled people concerning their military careers. He had a sign posted on his bulletin board that read: "Reenlistment Is Not A Right, It Is A Privilege."

What he was saying is that no one could demand the right to reenlist. This was a privilege that was EARNED through hard work, good conduct, and keeping a clean record. I saw many people denied reenlistment during my time in the Air Force due to a lack of these things. Jesus Christ did all of the "work" that you and I will ever need to get any blessing from God. Therefore since Jesus did this work on our behalf, you and I have a right to partake of the results of that work.

In our criminal justice system, people have rights. They do not earn these rights because of conduct. Most of them do not deserve these rights. Nevertheless the rights are made available to them and they can demand them.

The gospel does not just provide us with privileges. As the children of Abraham based upon the covenant of Abraham, we have RIGHTS. Jesus illustrates this point in the healing of the woman with a spirit of infirmity:

> *"And ought not this woman, BEING A DAUGHTER OF ABRAHAM, whom Satan hath bound, lo, these eighteen years, be loosed on the sabbath day?"* (Luke 13:16)

The word "ought" is used to express obligation, natural expectation, or logical consequence (Webster's Dictionary). Webster's Collegiate Thesaurus shows us that another word for "ought" is "right." A. B. Simpson in his excellent **Christ In The Bible Commentary** says:

> "This word 'should' [ought] expresses much more than willingness. It expresses obligation, right, something which it would be wrong not to do. It places divine healing on a very high and solid plane as not only a possible and actual intervention of God for the help of his suffering children, but as his normal provision for the believer. It is something that is included in our redemption rights, something that is part of the gospel of his grace, something that is already recognized as within His will and not requiring a special revelation to justify us in claiming it. If God expects us to do what we ought to do, surely we may expect as much from him."{2}

This woman had a legal right to healing because she was a daughter of Abraham. As we have seen, those of us who are born again are of the seed of Abraham and therefore we have the same covenant rights to healing.

Before the cross Satan had a legal right to destroy man's body. However, when Jesus atoned for our sins Satan lost all rights over us. The cross destroyed all of Satan's legal rights over us. Now the child of God has a right to all that God has made available.

During another time in Jesus' earthly ministry He showed a gentile woman that only those who were in covenant with God had a right to divine healing:

> *Then Jesus went thence, and departed into the coasts of Tyre and Sidon. And, behold, a woman of Canaan came out of the same coasts, and cried unto him, saying, Have mercy on me, O Lord, thou son of David; my daughter is grievously vexed with a devil. But he answered her not a word. And his disciples came and besought him, saying, Send her away; for she crieth after us. But he answered and said, I am not sent but unto the lost sheep of the house of Israel. Then came she and worshipped him, saying, Lord, help me. But he*

answered and said, **It is not meet to take the children's bread, and cast it to dogs.** *And she said, Truth, Lord: yet the dogs eat of the crumbs which fall from their masters' table. Then Jesus answered and said unto her, O woman, great is thy faith: be it unto thee even as thou wilt. And her daughter was made whole from that very hour.* (Matt. 15:21-28)

Jesus points out the fact that divine healing is the children's bread. That means it belongs to anyone who is a child of Abraham as a result of faith in Jesus Christ (John 8:39-44). Even greater than that, you are a child of God Himself. The children in my house have a right to the food that I provide for them. I would be arrested and thrown in jail if I denied my children their right. Yet we think that God, who is a greater Father than any human father would want us to beg and plead Him for something He has already provided.

God loves us and has made the living bread available to us. This bread is divine healing. We have the right to partake of it. God does not deny us of this right but encourages us to claim it by faith. Satan on the other hand would love for you to remain ignorant of this covenant right

There are two reasons why Satan does not want you to know that you have rights. The first reason is that if you believe that God's blessings are only PRIVILEGES (in the modern use of the word) then you will be reluctant to claim them. You will have the attitude that "If God wants to give it to me then He will in His own good time." This is not faith - it is laziness. Believing you only have privileges and not rights will prevent you from taking the bold action that is necessary to appropriate your healing. You will be under constant condemnation because you keep coming short of earning the privilege.

However, Satan knows that when you know that the Gospel benefits are your rights and that they belong to you then you will demand your right to be healed in Jesus Name. These demands are not to God - He wants you to have it. It is the devil who is stubborn and will not release you from the sickness until you take a bold stand against him. You must demand your right to be loosed from his grip.

The Bible shows us that all of God's promises are bound by covenant:

"But now hath he obtained a more excellent ministry, by how much also he is the mediator of a better covenant, which was established upon better promises." (Heb. 8:6)

When God makes a covenant with man He binds Himself to fulfill the promises and conditions of that covenant:

"My covenant will I not break, nor alter the thing that is gone out of my lips." (Ps. 89:34)

God knows that man needs something to keep his faith steady. If God were truly the wavering wishy washy God some of our theologians make him out to be, we could have no faith (i.e., God may heal sometimes in His own good time according to His sovereign will).

God wants man to understand what a covenant is. When we see that a covenant CANNOT be broken and we have in clear language what God promises to do as result of His covenant then our faith will be steadfast and we will boldly claim the fulfillment of the promise in Jesus name.

When you understand covenant you will know that it is no longer just a matter of God's sovereign will. You will see that He is obligated to fulfill the promises of His covenant.

Because of His holy and righteous nature, God cannot break His covenant which includes divine healing. He will not alter nor change His mind concerning His healing promises. God has given to us a covenant of healing:

*And said, If thou wilt diligently hearken to the voice of the LORD thy God, and wilt do that which is right in his sight, and wilt give ear to his commandments, and keep all his statutes, I will put none of these diseases upon thee, which I have brought upon the Egyptians: for **I am the LORD that healeth thee**.* (Ex. 15:26)

This is Jehovah Rophe - the Lord that healeth thee. This was one of God's many covenant names (Ex. 2:24; 6:1-6). This name reveals what God has bound Himself to do on behalf of His people when the conditions of the covenant have been fulfilled.

The name *"I am"* is a memorial to all generations (Ex. 3:14). In other words this name was to put us in remembrance of the covenant that God established with our forefathers. The revelation of Himself by this name revealed that He had the ability to become to His people whatever their needs required. It was an all-inclusive name. God was declaring, "I will be to you whatever you need."

My close friend, Dr. J. R. Roper says this in his book, My Covenant Memorial Name: I Am:

> "The Hebrew word for "AM" is 'hayah' (haw yaw): it is a primitive root structure and simply means to become, to exist or to be, to come to pass. It is always emphatic. Emphasis is always given to 'AM', regardless of how one uses AM. Things will exist, be, become or come to pass, simply because it is law."

Dr. Roper goes on to say:

> "When 'I AM' is used by covenant people the tendency to become whatever is said is set in motion."{3}

This is some wonderful and practical advice from a man of God. We apply God's covenant rights to our lives by the power of confession. Satan wants us to focus on the physical circumstances and make confessions such as "I AM sick." This is invoking the covenant in the wrong manner and revoking our covenant rights. We must use God's covenant name positively by saying "I AM healed by the stripes of Jesus."

Confession is vital to receiving your covenant rights. Confession is an act of faith. It is saying the same thing that God says about your situation. Abraham, when desiring healing so that he would be able to produce a child did not "consider his own body" (Rom.

4:19). He continued to confess the promise of God for him by taking the name "Abraham" which meant "father of many nations."

One of the things that happens in a covenant is that you take the name of the person that you enter into covenant with. When Abram entered into covenant with God he took the name ABRAHAM. The "AH" came from the name "Jehovah". Whenever he introduced himself as Abraham he was making a confession: "I AM the father of many nations. Sarai took the name SARAH. She too took part of the name of Jehovah. Whenever she called herself that she confessed, "I AM the mother of many nations" (see Genesis 17). Notice also that they took these names BEFORE they saw any physical manifestation.

The closest thing to a covenant that we now have in the western world is marriage. God calls marriage a covenant (Mal. 2:14). When I married my wife Takako we entered into covenant with one another. One of the first things she did was take on my name. She was no longer Miss Takako Uchima. She is now Mrs. Takako Edwards. Whenever she introduces herself to others she is confessing, "I am Troy Edwards wife."

Since you and I have entered into covenant with God by being BORN AGAIN into His family by the blood of Jesus we have no business taking on our maiden names of "sickness, poverty, and lack." Jehovah Rophe - I am the Lord that healeth thee is His covenant name. This is the name we must take.

Instead of saying, "I AM sick" when you are being attacked with sickness, you should confess "I AM healed," thereby confessing the name of the covenant that you are very much a part of. Just as a wife would take the last name of her covenant partner (her husband) to make the fact that she is married to him

more of a reality, so must you take the name of "I am the Lord that healeth thee" so that the truth of this will become more of a reality in your physical body.

You and I must learn to confess what God says and not what circumstances say. The only way to claim your rights in Christ is by making a proper confession. If we are going to continually use God's covenant name in a negative confession (I AM sick) then we will get the results thereof. We must learn to invoke this covenant name of healing and walk in divine health.

Satan knows this and will continually try to get you to revoke your covenant rights through a negative confession. He will get you focused on your suffering and pain instead of believing what God's word says. You must learn to study your covenant and become familiar with its promises. Only then will you be able to speak forth your covenant rights.

We should become familiar with the Scriptures that mention the covenant name of Jehovah. These Scriptures will tell you rights you have as a result of your covenant.

One of the many Scriptures can be found in Psalms 91:

> *"He that dwelleth in the secret place of the most High shall abide under the shadow of the Almighty. I WILL SAY of the Lord, He is my refuge and my fortress: my God; in him will I trust."* (Ps. 91:1-2)

The name "almighty" is Shaddai which means the all sufficient one. The One Who is more than enough to supply your needs. The name "Lord" is the name "Jehovah" which we have just told you means covenant keeping God.

Notice the confession, *"I will say of Jehovah....."* Whatever Jehovah has promised to be to us, we must confess it so that it will be so in our lives. The Psalmist here is confessing Jehovah as his refuge. Jehovah is a refuge from sickness and disease. Read verses 3 through 6 of this Psalm:

> *Surely he shall deliver thee from the snare of the fowler, and from the noisome pestilence. He shall cover thee with his feathers, and under his wings shalt thou trust: his truth shall be thy shield and buckler. Thou shalt not be afraid for the terror by night; nor for the arrow that flieth by day; Nor for the pestilence that walketh in darkness; nor for the destruction that wasteth at noonday.*

Now read how the Everyday Bible translates the above verses: *"God will save you from hidden traps and from* **deadly diseases**. *He will protect you like a bird spreading it's wings over its young. His truth will be like your armor and shield. You will not fear any danger by night nor an arrow during the day.* **You will not be afraid of diseases that come in the dark or sickness that strikes at noon.***"*

Jehovah through His covenant has promise to save and protect us from deadly diseases. Because we have covenant with God we need not ever fear sickness and disease. Isn't that good news. It does not matter that your family has a history of asthma, cancer, high blood pressure, or any other kind of sickness. These things must stop with the one who has entered into covenant with God.

Verses 9 and 10 of Psalm 91 go on to say:

"Because thou hast made the Lord [Jehovah - the covenant keeping God], which is my refuge, even the most High, thy habitation; THERE SHALL NO EVIL BEFALL THEE, neither shall any plague come nigh thy dwelling."

Remember in Deuteronomy 7:15 we saw that God called diseases "evil." God has covenanted with us to be our refuge from sickness and disease. He will ensure that NO EVIL, which includes the evil diseases mentioned in Deuteronomy 7:15 will befall us (Ex. 23:25). I have claimed this particular promise on many occasions when my family was attacked with sickness.

Sickness is evil. God promises that sickness will not befall thee. A plague is a type of sickness. God promises that it will not come near your dwelling. When sickness does manage to attack my wife or children I always remind it of this Scripture. I tell it that it should not be near my dwelling so it must leave. My dwelling is my home and so is yours. Again, God has always been faithful to fulfill this promise. This is our covenant right in Christ.

Many times Bible teachers liken our redemption to the Emancipation Proclamation that Lincoln used to free the black slaves from the white masters after the civil war. Though many of these slaves enjoyed their freedom to a certain extent, they were ignorant of another document called THE BILL OF RIGHTS. The Emancipation Proclamation told them that they were free but the Bill of Rights told them what was right fully theirs.

Because of this ignorance, many of these former slaves were still oppressed by the white man. Even though they were free they did not know how to stay free of oppression because they did not know their rights. This ignorance kept them from claiming all that was made available to them as American citizens.

Many Christians have been freed from Satan's kingdom by accepting Christ as their savior (Col. 1:12-14). Yet they are still oppressed by sickness, disease, sin, poverty, fear, etc. This is due to an ignorance of their rights. We need not suffer any sickness or disease. It is not the will of God and neither is it His desire for you. He has given you a covenant with many promises contained therein that you have the right to claim. Do not let Satan oppress you with sickness. It is your God given right to be healed.

Chapter Seven

Healing Glorifies God

"So God's blessings are given to us by faith, as a free gift, WE ARE CERTAIN TO GET THEM....." (Rom. 4:16; Living Bible)

So far we have taught six indisputable truths concerning divine healing that, if meditated upon and applied, will guarantee your healing. Yet there is one more truth concerning divine healing that is necessary for you to know, and that is that divine healing brings God glory. It glorifies Him.

There are those who oppose ministers that proclaim the truth concerning God's material and physical blessings. They believe that this type of teaching produces selfish Christians. They believe that a Christian who desires healing does not know how to "suffer for Christ."

There is a suffering for Christ that will bring Him glory (1 Pet. 4:14-16). Those who will live godly in Christ Jesus will suffer persecution (2 Tim. 3:12). These things are inevitable. Nevertheless, we must remember that it is not the suffering itself that brings God the glory, but our attitude in it.

Those who promote the "suffering for Christ" doctrine always neglect to tell us one thing: That God promises to DELIVER us from our trials and persecutions (Psalm 34:19; Isa. 43:2; Dan. 3:19-25; 6:19-23; John 16:33). The Scriptures, however, make this clear. In fact, it is this deliverance that will glorify Him (Psalm 50:14, 15; Isa. 25:1-5).

However, Christ did not once tell his disciples nor us that we had to suffer sickness. Suffering trials, tribulations, and persecutions for the sake of the gospel does not mean allowing sickness to destroy us. The Bible makes a clear distinction in God's attitude towards suffering sickness and suffering persecution:

"Is anyone among you afflicted (ill treated, suffering evil)? He should pray. Is anyone glad at heart? He

should sing praise [to God]" (James 5:13; Amplified Bible)

I used the Amplified translation to show you that the actual word *afflicted* in verse 13 has nothing to do with sickness. Wuest's says it this way: *"Is anyone among you suffering misfortune? Let him keep on constantly praying."* Other translations use the word *"troubles"* in place of afflicted. Then we go to verse 14 and 15 which says:

> *"Is any sick among you? Let him call for the elders of the church: and let them pray over him, anointing him with oil in the name of the Lord: AND THE PRAYER OF FAITH SHALL SAVE THE SICK......"*

Verses 14 and 15 are a continuation of the thought being conveyed in verse 13. Therefore it is easy to see that the author is making a distinction between the suffering of trials and the suffering of sickness. Though God will deliver us from trials, the only instruction here for that is prayer. We are not to oppose those who are persecuting us. We are to pray for them (Matt. 5:44).

However, sickness is not to be tolerated. We are to oppose it. We are to take action against it. Sickness is an evil that God does not want us to tolerate. By not opposing those who persecute us and cause us problems, we may win them or those around us to Christ. Nevertheless, this cannot be true of sickness and disease. God desires that we pray the prayer of faith which will destroy it.

Suffering persecution and standing up against it with boldness brings glory to God. Suffering sickness does not. There is no Scripture that anyone can find to prove this. There is no case in history where the actual sickness brought glory to God. Opposing the sickness by faith and receiving deliverance is what brings glory to God.

There are some beautiful saints of God who, because of ignorance concerning divine healing or a refusal to believe this portion of the gospel, have learned to glorify God through their lives in spite of their handicaps. God overruled the handicap and blessed them with gifts and talents that have encouraged and blessed others. Some of them have even won others to Christ. However, it was not the handicap that glorified God. It was their perseverance in spite of the handicap.

As wonderful and beautiful as these precious saints were (or are), they did not receive the best that God has for them. This does not mean that they are not precious in God's sight. I would never imply that. This does not mean that they do not have great rewards awaiting them in heaven. On the contrary, many of these people probably have an abundance awaiting their homecoming.

Still, we want to show you that the receiving of physical blessings also glorifies God.

What do we mean by *"glorifying God"* or *"Giving God the glory"*? According to W. E. Vines it means *"to magnify extol, praise.... ascribing honor to Him, acknowledging Him as to His being, attributes and acts."*{1}

In Psalms God shows us very simply what it means to glorify Him:

"Whoso offereth praise glorifieth me....." (Ps. 50:23)

The glorifying of God is expressed in our praise to Him. We offer praise as we sing, shout, and dance with joy. I have heard people say, "I thank you for the sickness God. I thank you for the trials," but there was no joy in it. They mumbled this prayer as though it was an obligation. The truth is, they do not really mean it.

The truth is that they know in their hearts that sickness and trials are nothing to praise God about. This is just something that they have been taught to do. Really, they are not happy because they think God put it on them. God gets no glory from this.

Whatever will cause men to think highly of God, whatever, will cause men to see the truth about God, whatever will draw men and women to the true and living God, whatever will cause men to have faith in God, is that which glorifies Him. Again Vines says, *"As the glory of God is the revelation and manifestation of all that He has and is..., it is said of a Self-revelation in which God manifests all the goodness that is His."* {2}

Glorifying God is giving God the attention He is due because of His goodness, love, and by the plain fact that He is God. Whenever people in church, be it a preacher, musician, choir soloist, etc. use their talents, gifts and abilities to draw attention to themselves, they are not glorifying God, but themselves. That was the problem with Satan and this was the cause of his downfall.

Now that we know what it means to glorify God we should have a better understanding of the fact that healing and not sickness is what brings Him this glory. There are several Bible references that prove this (Matt. 15:29-31; Luke 5:17-26; 18:35-43; John 9:1-7; 11:3-6, 39-45 Acts 3:1-10, 4:21-22). Let us examine why healing glorifies Him.

1. Healing Shows God's Love And Mercy Towards Man

In Luke 5:17-26 a paralyzed man was brought in through the roof of the house where Jesus was teaching. This man desired healing. The first thing Jesus told him was that his sins were forgiven him. The Pharisees did not like this. They felt that only God could forgive sins. They did not realize that Jesus was God manifested in a physical body.

Jesus decided to prove that He had power to forgive sins. The best way to prove it was to heal the man. The man received his healing and we read:

> *"And immediately he rose up before them, and took up that whereon he lay, and departed to his house, GLORIFYING GOD. And they were all amazed, AND THEY GLORIFIED GOD....."* (Luke 5:25-26a)

God forgives us out of His love and mercy. Obviously this man must have sinned somehow to get in this condition. Nonetheless, Jesus removed all condemnation of sin by forgiving him. This put this man in a position of faith to receive healing.

We all deserve the penalty that comes with the broken law which is death, sickness, and poverty. However, God out of His abundant love and mercy not only forgives us and releases us from our sins by the shed blood of Christ, but He also releases us from its penalty.

God is not glorified when He is portrayed as a cruel task master who punishes people with some kind of disease for angering Him. What draws people to God is His love and His mercy, the demonstration of His goodness toward us in spite of our failures.

2. It Proves That God Gets No Joy From The Suffering Of Others

Jesus was teaching in the synagogues on the Sabbath day and a woman with a spirit of infirmity was there. Jesus called her to him,

> *"And he laid his hands on her: and immediately she was made straight, and GLORIFIED GOD."* (Luke 13:13).

When the ruler of the synagogue became indignant concerning the Sabbath day healing Jesus answered:

> *"....Thou hypocrite, doth not each one of you on the sabbath loose his ox or his ass from the stall, and lead him away to watering? And ought not this woman, being a daughter of Abraham, whom Satan has bound, lo, these eighteen years, be loosed from this bond on the sabbath day."* (Luke 13:15, 16)

Jesus showed them that if they cared so much about the suffering of their animals that have no covenant, then surely God cares much more for His suffering children. They received no pleasure from seeing one of their animals fall into a ditch. Just the same, God receives no pleasure from any of His children suffering sickness. This should be a spike in the heart of all modern theology that teaches that God gets pleasure and is glorified by His children suffering sickness.

3. It Demonstrates God's Power Over That Of Satan's.

This same account in Luke also demonstrates how God's power far exceeds that of Satan's. God is full of love and goodness and desires nothing but the best for His creation. Satan is full of cruelty and hatred and wants nothing more than to steal, to kill, and to destroy. Who would you rather have the greater power? God or Satan?

The God of all goodness had the power and ability to loose this woman from Satan's bondage. Satan could not stand against the power of God. This shows that when we are on God side and walking in His ways we have no choice but to be victorious. We are walking in the power of the One whose power far exceeds that of our adversary.

The people who were present were so amazed with what was done:

".....and all the people REJOICED for all the glorious things that were done by him." (Luke 13:17b)

They did not rejoice at the bondage in which Satan had placed this woman. They rejoiced at how the power of God overcame that of Satan's. People want to be free, not bound. <u>When people see a power that is greater than the one oppressing them then they will want to be a partaker of it.</u>

4. It Draws Men To Christ

I have never seen people run to God to receive sickness. I have never seen one account in the Bible teaching such a thing. Yet many in the evangelical church believe that they can win the unsaved world by telling them that God either does not heal today or that He MAY heal if it's His will but you have no GUARANTEE.

It's no wonder that we are having such a hard time winning the world to Jesus. Personally, I am weary of the "occasional" soul being saved. In the book of Acts we see something better. We see multitudes being added to the Lord.

In Acts 3:1-10 God used Peter and John to minister healing to a cripple man. The his healing led him to glorifying God:

> *"And he leaping up stood, and walked, and entered with them into the temple, walking, and leaping, and PRAISING God. And all the people saw him walking and praising God."* (Acts 3:8, 9)

This man began praising and glorifying God for the healing. He had something to praise God for. Even better, the people saw it and were amazed and filled with wonderment (v. 10). This gave Peter an opportunity to tell them the good news of Jesus Christ. Look at the results of that:

> *"Howbeit many of them which heard the word believed; and the number of the men was about five thousand."* (Acts 4:4)

That's quite a number of people to receive salvation due to one man's preaching. Peter had physical, living, and material proof that Jesus was alive. He had a man that everyone knew was a hopeless cripple. They saw a genuine miracle of healing.

Of course the devil did not like it and brought them persecution from the religious leaders. It's the same thing that happens in our day. They could threaten these men of God but could not stop them nor could they deny the genuineness of this healing. This healing brought glory to God and shame to the devil.

> *".....for all men GLORIFIED GOD for that which was done. For the man was above forty years old, on whom this miracle of healing was shewed."* (Acts 4:21-22)

Why did they glorify God? For that which was done. What was done? The healing of a forty year old cripple. At that age you know that most of the people knew this man and knew that this was no fake. It was genuine.

True evangelism is not done with methods only, but with POWER. We can talk and argue with people all day long but when people see the Word of God demonstrated then they are drawn. Healing glorifies God by drawing men and women to Him:

> *"And believers were the more added to the Lord, multitudes both of men and women. Insomuch that they brought forth the sick into the streets, and laid them on beds and couches, that at the least the shadow of Peter passing by might overshadow some of them. There came a certain multitude out of the cities round about Jerusalem, bringing sick folks, and them which had unclean spirits: and they were healed every one."* (Acts 5:14-16)

We need this kind of power working in the church today if we want our churches full. This is not so that we can compete in having the largest congregations, but because we have a genuine concern for the lost. These men walked in power. This same power is available today if we would just believe and walk in it. However, our intentions for doing so should be to glorify God.

5. It's Proof That God Answers Prayer

Healing of the body is one of the best proofs that God is a prayer answering God. On His way to Jericho, a blind man cried out to Jesus. Jesus had the man brought to Him and asked Him what was it that he needed (Though God knows our needs we still must be specific with Him). The man requested that he may receive his sight. Jesus tells the blind man that his faith has done it for him:

"And immediately he received his sight, and followed him, GLORIFYING GOD: and ALL the people, when they saw it, GAVE PRAISE TO GOD." (Luke 5:43)

God wants us to come to Him with our needs. He desires to answer our prayers. It is these prayers of faith based on His promises that bring Him glory (Dan. 2:16-23; John 14:13-14; 2 Cor. 1:20-22). When people see that God truly answers prayer then they will want to get to know that God.

God does not say no to our prayers if they are based on His covenant promises to us (2 Cor. 1:20-22). We have seen throughout these lessons that healing is a promise that can be appropriated by faith and prayer. When we pray and receive healing we demonstrate to others that God is not a liar but He is true and faithful to His Word. This glorifies Him.

Healing glorifies God. Therefore appropriating healing for our sick bodies is not something selfish. We want to show the world that our God is real. Therefore receive your healing and be a testimony for God's glory.

Chapter Eight

How To Appropriate Healing

We have given you seven indisputable truths concerning divine healing. We have shown you exactly what the Bible says about healing. This should have built a foundation for faith.

Now we want to show you seven practical steps that will enable you to appropriate the healing that you need or the protection from sickness that you desire. I like to call these "steps for those who do not know any better." The reason for this is that we do not want to imply that these steps are the only way to be healed.

We have no desire to put God in a box or regulate the blessings of God to a standard formula. It cannot be done. We do not want people becoming mechanical. God wants a relationship with His children and does not want to be a vending machine of blessings just because we followed the right steps.

However, laws of the Spirit work just the same as those in the natural realm. There are certain procedures to follow in the natural realm and you will find the same thing in the spirit realm.

Some people recognize that it is God's will to heal but do not receive because they do not know exactly how to appropriate. That is why we offer these steps. God will honor you where you begin. Once you have learned these steps and have developed your faith and relationship with God then appropriating healing will come natural to you. Until this is done, one must start somewhere and therefore we have offered these practical steps.

1. Find The Scriptures That Promise Healing And Meditate On Them

The reason many people do not receive healing is because they neglect to find out for themselves what God's word has to say about it. They will hear those who preach against it and accept their opinion. They may even hear those like myself who preaches for it and accepts our word. However, it is not sufficient to accept what I say or what another says. You must know what God says about it Himself.

Psalms shows us that the provision for healing was sent to us by God's Word:

> *"He sent his word, and healed them, and delivered them from their destructions."* (Ps. 107:20)

If the provision for healing comes by God's Word, doesn't it make sense to find out exactly what His word has to say on the subject. Jesus, who is God manifested in the flesh spoke the word and brought healing (Matt. 8:5-8, 16). He was here to DO the will of God and He only SAID those things His Father told Him to say. Therefore Jesus applied the Word of God in His healing ministry.

Just as there are those who are ignorant concerning the Word of God towards healing, there are others who do know what it says but do not meditate upon it. Yet, this is also essential to receiving healing:

> *"My son, attend to my words; incline thine ear unto my sayings. Let them not depart from thine eyes; KEEP THEM IN THE MIDST OF THINE HEART. For they are LIFE unto those that find them, AND HEALTH TO ALL THEIR FLESH."* (Prov. 4:20-22).

God's Word is life. It will overcome the death and destruction that is come to destroy your body. His words are health to all your flesh. No one can say anything about "spiritual healing" here. This is making it plain and clear that bodily health is the subject. We must learn to find out what the Word says about it and meditate on that.

Mental acknowledgment of God's Word is a good place to start but it must not stop there. The key is to get it in the midst of your heart. This is where true faith operates to appropriate healing for the body (Mark 11:22-24; Rom. 10:8-10). Meditating on the word is the key to doing it. This passage explains exactly how to mediate on God's Word: By placing it first, by listening to it with your inner ear, and by never letting it depart from before you.

2. Pray The Prayer Of Faith

In the book of James we are told exactly what means God will use to save the sick:

"And THE PRAYER OF FAITH shall save the sick, and the Lord shall raise him up...." (James 5:15)

It is not the elders praying over him and anointing him with oil that will save the sick. This is one of the vehicles that God may use to bring forth healing. The Bible is clear that the *prayer of faith* is what saves the sick and moves the Lord to raise him up.

This faith comes by the hearing and hearing of God's Word (Rom. 10:17). If you did the first step then you will have no problem with this step. There are several instances in the Bible where Jesus commends people for their faith. It was their display of faith that opened the door for God to manifest His healing power in their bodies.

One night after teaching a Bible class at a church I once attended I had several people come to ask questions. One man asked, "If I pray for a sinner will that sinner get healed by my faith or will the person have to have faith for his or her self?"

Before I could answer the question another couple that was beside me blurted out, "It's not your faith that gets people healed, it's God that does the healing." I turned around and quietly explained to them that faith is involved in the healing process with one exception, the gifts of healing being in operation. When the gifts of healing are being manifested the recipient need not have faith. Then I turned back around to the first man and answered his question.

Sometimes we can get so caught up in terminology and play on words that we miss the Spirit of God. This is because if the Holy Spirit is not moving according to our theological terms then it cannot be Him (So we think).

Nevertheless, prayer prayed in faith is a sure guarantee of receiving your healing. This prayer is based on the fact that you that

God did not lie about His promises and that He is faithful to perform them.

3. Praise God For The Healing Before And After It's Manifestation

The prayer of faith believes that it receives before any physical evidence has manifested (Mark 11:24). Notice the prayer of David for healing:

> *"Have mercy upon me, O Lord; for I am weak: O Lord, heal me; for my bones are vexed."* (Ps. 6:2)

First David makes several requests to God including healing. There is nothing wrong with petitioning our heavenly Father for anything and most certainly we may request healing based on His promises to do so. However, the prayer of faith does not stop with its petition. It walks away believing that it has been heard and answered:

> *"The Lord HATH HEARD my supplication; the Lord will receive my prayer."* (Ps. 6:9)

If God hears and receives our prayers then you can be sure that He has answered it (1 Pet. 3:12; 1 John 5:14-15; John 11:41-44; Ps. 34:4-9; Prov. 21:13). David walked away with confidence that His prayer was heard and received. His statement was one of confidence.

If we truly believe that God has heard our prayer then we will thank and praise Him. Phillipians 4:6 tells us that "thanksgiving" must ACCOMPANY our petitions. It does not wait until we have physical evidence.

Praising and thanking God for your healing in spite of contradicting evidence is a true demonstration of faith. Nevertheless, many would rather wait until AFTER they have the physical feeling to praise God. This is not the Bible order:

"Let the people praise thee, O God; let all the people praise thee. THEN shall the earth yield her increase; and God, even our own God shall bless us." (Ps. 67:5, 6)

The word "then" is used to show what is to happen in a specific order. In other words if you do this THEN you will get the results thereof. "Then" shows a pattern that must be followed. Therefore we must praise God first in order to see His blessings manifest. Praise first and then blessings. No praise, no blessings. Praise God for the healing in spite of how you feel and THEN you will receive the feeling.

4. Continually Confess The Promises

Along with praise we must confess what God says about our situation and not what the situation looks like. This is another area where many people miss it. They ask God for healing but if it has not manifested right away then they make statements contrary to God's Word such as: "I'm still sick."

If God said that you were healed (1 Pet. 2:24) and you have asked for this promise to be made real in your body then you should not speak contrary to the truth. God's word is the truth and everything else should be considered a lie (John 17:17).

The Bible shows us that our tongues make the difference between life and death in our physical bodies:

"Death and life are in the power of the tongue...." (Prov. 18:21)

Your words give you the choice of receiving from God or from the devil. Sickness as we explained earlier is the result of death. Life comes from God and will be manifested in your mortal body by the Holy Spirit if you speak the Word (Rom. 8:11).

Our words must agree with God's words even when everything seems contrary to it. We are fighting a good fight of faith and the only way to lay hold to eternal life which will manifest itself in our bodies is to confess a good confession (1 Tim. 6:12). So in the midst of your battle for healing hold fast to your confession of God's promise of healing (Heb. 10:23).

5. Resist All Attacks And Lies That Come From Satan And Others.

Anything that speaks contrary to the Word of God is a lie from Satan (John 8:44). Any theology that opposes divine healing is a lie from him. Yet, you will not know this unless you have first taken step one which is to find the promises of God concerning healing and meditate on them.

Satan will oppose you and try you. He will do it by speaking to your mind and telling you, "you're going to die. You'll never be healed." He may send well meaning friends and relatives to convince you that you are being foolish. They may even tell you about some friend who believed God for healing and they died. However, you must resist all opposition that Satan brings against you:

> *"Submit yourselves therefore to God. Resist the devil and he will flee from you."* (James 4:7)

How do you submit yourself to God? By submitting to the authority of His Word. You accept what the Word of God says on the subject of healing and not what the devil or well meaning (and not so well meaning) people have to say about it. How do you resist the devil? The same way Jesus did, by using God's Word against him (Matt. 4:1-11; Eph. 6:17).

You must be prepared to take the healing promises and use them against the devil and all demon forces. The promise given to us is that "he will flee from you." He will not just quietly walk away - he will FLEE. The promises of God cut through his lies and he can't stand that. Stand on God's Word and watch the devil run.

6. Don't Give Up Even When The Healing Hasn't Manifested Right Away.

This is an important step. In the midst of pain we all would rather die and be relieved. However, your desire should be for the glory of God as we have seen in our previous lesson. Giving up will not glorify God. Standing in faith until your healing manifests will give you a testimony that will bring glory to God, build the faith of others and shut the mouths of God's enemies.

Jesus encourages that when we pray, we should not give up:

> *"Also [Jesus] told them a parable to the effect that they ought always to pray and not to turn coward (faint, lose heart, and give up)."* (Luke 18:1; Amplified Bible).

Remember we said that standing in faith for healing was a fight. Sometimes the devil may even increase the pain and have the doctor give worse medical reports on you. Yet Jesus encourages that once we have made our prayer of petition that we should not turn coward and give up. Do not let the pain or medical reports scare you from the healing that is rightfully yours. Hold fast to your confession without wavering (Heb. 10:23).

Again, you must remember that Satan is the source of all sickness. So when you are fighting in faith against it you are in essence fighting against the devil himself. He has no desire for God to get any glory. He wants you to stay sick. He will even kill you off if he can. You will make the difference as to whether God gets any glory in your situation or not.

The Bible tells us to stand firm against all satanic attacks:

> *"Withstand him; be firm in faith [against his onset-rooted, established, strong, immovable, and determined]."* (1 Pet. 5:9; Amplified Bible)

"Stand firm when he attacks. Trust the Lord...." (1 Pet. 5:9; Living Bible)

"Refuse to give in to the devil. Stand strong in your faith." (The Everyday Bible).

Keep standing in faith and trust the Lord for the manifestation of your healing. Remember that God's power is greater than that of the devil. It will be your steadfast faith that puts this power in to operation in your body.

7. Repent Of Any Known Sin In Your Life.

Though it is not always the case, sickness can sometimes be the result of some sin in our lives. People do not realize that unforgiveness, bitterness, strife, sexual sins, and many other things open the door for Satan to attack. Nonetheless, many Scriptures in the Bible prove this to be true.

Jeremiah 5:25 tells us that it is sin that withholds good things from us. Now healing is a very good thing, especially when you are sick. Isaiah 59:1, 2 tells us that God does not hear and answer prayer due to sin. Proverbs 28:13 tells us that when we cover our sins we will not prosper. Healing is a form of physical prosperity. Thank God that proverbs 28:13 does not stop there, it says that when we CONFESS and FORSAKE our sins we shall have mercy.

James shows us that this mercy manifests itself in physical healing:

"And the prayer of faith shall save the sick, and the Lord shall raise him up; and if he have committed sins, they shall be forgiven him." (James 5:14)

James shows us not only the guaranteed promise of physical healing, but also the guarantee that any sins that resulted in the sickness will be forgiven. This is nothing but the love and mercy of

Almighty God. However, if we read on, we find that there is a condition to receiving the forgiveness that leads to healing:

"Confess your faults one to another, and pray for one another that you may be healed. The effectual fervent prayer of a RIGHTEOUS man availeth much."

Confessing our faults is an important process to healing. When we confess, we are more reluctant to do that thing again. The confession of sin must be accompanied with full repentance. We must determine to turn from that sin and never go back to it.

Sin causes us to lose our right standing with God. An unrighteous man has no guarantee that God will answer his prayer unless it is one of repentance. Once sin has been repented of the person is automatically made righteous again by the blood of Jesus (1 John 1:7-9).

Once we have become righteous again then our prayer for healing will avail much with God. We will break through the barrier that was caused by sin and we will receive the healing that we desire.

Apply these seven steps and God will manifest His healing.

Chapter Nine

How To Minister Healing To The Sick

So far the truths that we have shared with you may have blessed you tremendously. You may now have no problems appropriating healing for yourself. However, you may know someone who is sick and you desire to minister healing to them but you do not know how.

First of all you do not necessarily need to bring them to church and have the pastor lay hands on them. They might be dead before the next Sunday service. You need not bother the pastor to go to the person's house or the hospital to do it. He may be busy enough ministering to others in the congregation.

You need not wait until the next healing evangelist comes to town. The person might be dead before then too. What I am trying to tell you is YOU CAN MINISTER HEALING TO THE SICK. Yes, my friend, God can use you. You need not be an apostle, prophet, evangelist, pastor, or teacher. God said that the ministry of healing was for ALL Believers (Mark 16:15-20).

If you do not know how to do it then this chapter was written to offer you some assistance. However, remember what was stated in the last lesson. The principles that we offer here are not the standard formula. These are written to get you STARTED until you have progressed to the point where you can hear from God and He can lead you in different ways to minister to people. However, God will honor your present level of faith.

It is not necessary for others to suffer and die just because you are not a the level of fellowship with God that you think you should be. Take what we offer you here and God will honor His Word. However, always remember that God desires that you grow in relationship with Him so that He Himself can lead in different ways to minister healing to the sick.

1. Recognize That We Are Depending On God To Do The Healing And Not Ourselves.

Sometimes we get a little worried about ministering to the sick because it might hurt our reputation if the person does not recover. It makes us look bad. On the other hand, when we have had some significant success in seeing people healed as a result of our ministering to them our ego swells to the size of a Good Year blimp.

When we recognize that it is totally up to God to perform the healing and not us then this will save us from disappointment and it will also save us from being proud. Peter makes it clear who did the healing in the case of the cripple at the gate.

> *"And when Peter saw it, he answered unto the people, Ye men of Israel, why marvel ye at this? or why look ye so earnestly on us, as though by our own power or holiness we had made this man to walk."* (Acts 3:12)

Some Bible commentators actually teach that the apostles healed the sick. Yet, Peter makes it clear that he had no personal power from himself to heal. It was not his great holiness that brought healing to the cripple. Peter goes on to teach them exactly how this healing was wrought:

> *"And His name through faith in his name hath made this man strong, whom ye see and know: yea, the faith which is by him hath given him this perfect soundness in the presence of you all."* (Acts 3:16).

It was faith that turned on the power of God and brought healing to the cripple. God's power is always present to heal:

> *".....and the power of the Lord was present to HEAL them."* (Luke 5:17)

So you and I are not responsible for doing the healing. It is faith in His power to heal. I personally believe that both the one doing the ministering and the one being ministered to must use faith. More than likely, since you are going to minister healing, your faith is already there. As we will see in the principles I have outlined, part of your ministry is to build the faith of the recipient. Both you and the sick one must remember that YOU are not going to heal - God is. You provide the means for receiving faith, God provides the healing. One cannot ask for a better deal.

2. You Must Build The Recipients Faith By Ministering The Word To Them.

Now that we see that it is faith that brings the ever present power of God into manifestation we must also see that part of ministering healing is building the person's faith. The only means of building a person's faith for healing is the Word of God (Rom. 10:17). Paul gives us a clear example of this.

Paul went to Lycaonia and preached the gospel (Acts 14:6, 7). The word "gospel" means good news. Healing is a part of the gospel message (Matt. 10:1-8; Luke 9:1-6; 10:1-9; Mark 16:15-20). The gospel is the Word of God (Col.1:5). There was a man who had been cripple from birth.

> *"The same heard Paul speak: who steadfastly beholding him, and perceiving that he had faith to be healed, Said with a loud voice, Stand upright on thy feet. And he leaped and walked."* (Acts 14:9, 10)

The Word that Paul was ministering gave this cripple faith to receive healing. That is why it is essential that we minister God's Word to people if they are to receive healing. If the gifts of the Spirit (1 Cor. 12) come into operation then there will be no need for any faith. The Holy Spirit will just heal.

Nevertheless this only happens as the Spirit wills (1 Cor. 12:11). At this point we can use God's sovereignty as a good reason.

There is no guarantee of the gifts of the Spirit operating to bring about a miraculous healing. It may and it may not happen.

However, the Word of God is always guaranteed to work if we will put our faith in it. So always minister the Word. We have shown you plenty of Scriptures in these lessons that you can give to the sick one. You might even give them this book to read or another good book on healing.

Also be sure to minister God's Word to them concerning forgiveness if there was any sin committed that may have led to the sickness. This may not always be the case so do not assume. James says *"IF he has committed sins, they shall be forgiven."* (James 5:15).

The word *"if"* in that passage shows that sickness is not always the result of a person having committed sin. Sickness is the result of sin in the world but not always the result of the individual.

However, if sin is involved in the sickness, you must first minister God's forgiveness to the person as Jesus did (Mark 2:1-12). Show them what the Bible has to say about forgiveness. Often, people cannot receive healing because they are under condemnation of sin. This condemnation is hindering their faith. They must know that God loves them and forgives them and desires to heal them. So sharing the Word is necessary to ministering healing.

3. Anoint With Oil If Possible

There was a time that I did not think that this was important. Later, I discovered the powerful truth concerning the holy anointing oil and I began to have a change of heart. James strongly encourages anointing the sick with oil:

> *"Is any sick among you? Let him call for the elders of the church; and let them pray over him, anointing him with oil in the name of the Lord."* (James 5:14)

This same truth is found in Mark 6:13:

"And they cast out many devils, and anointed with oil many that were sick, and healed them."

The oil was a type of the Holy Spirit. When the person was anointed with oil it represented the Holy Spirit coming upon the person's body to bring about the necessary healing (Rom. 8:11).

In Exodus 30:23-25 we find the origin of the anointing oil. When God gave Moses the instructions on how to make this oil, He told him exactly which spices to put in the oil. There was to be no substitutes. Each of the spices represented different aspects of the Holy Spirit's ministry.

One of the spices was pure myrrh. The word *pure* in this passage comes from the Hebrew word *derowr* (Strong's no. 1865) and it means *"freedom and liberty."* It is the same word that is associated with the year of Jubilee when all slaves were freed and everyone was loosed from their debts (Lev. 25:10; Isa. 61:1; Jer. 34:8-17; Ezek. 44:17).

God anoints us with the Holy Spirit to give freedom and liberty from all sickness and disease. Jesus was "anointed" of the Holy Ghost and He HEALED all that were oppressed by the devil. This is the Holy Spirit's ministry - to set us free from the oppression of sickness that Satan would put on our bodies.

The anointing, according to Isaiah, is what destroys the yoke of bondage (Isa. 10:24-27). The "yoke" mentioned in Isaiah was an arched device formerly laid on the neck of a defeated person. Sickness brings misery and defeat but the Holy Spirit anoints us to set us free and liberate us from that.

A good example was the cleansing of the Leper in Leviticus 14. First there was blood applied. God does not anoint us until we first partake of the blood of the atonement Christ wrought on our behalf. That is why James encourages the one seeking healing to confess his or her faults. It is by this that the blood is applied and sins are forgiven (1 John 1:7-9). Afterwards, the Levitcal priest applied the oil. When all of this was done, the leper was declared cleansed. This cleansing referred to in Leviticus meant complete healing (Luke 5:12-14).

James and the Christians of his day understood these truths better than anyone. When the sick person who understood this truth was anointed with oil, it VITALIZED HIS FAITH. It strengthened the recipient's faith because they knew that this represented the Holy Spirit coming upon their body to free them from the sickness, thereby bringing complete healing. That is why the next verse in James says:

> *"And the prayer of FAITH shall save the sick, and the Lord shall raise him up."* (James 5:15)

Notice that oil and prayer was applied together. The Holy Spirit is always available to heal, but it is our prayer offered in faith that puts His power into operation.

The oil is a type of the Holy Spirit and thus a faith builder. If you have anointing oil I highly recommend it's use. Nevertheless do not allow a lack of it to keep you from ministering to the sick. I have prayed for many without this oil and God has healed them. However, this oil is a faith builder and it can work to bring about healing.

4. Lay Hands On Them

Next you should lay hands on them and pray for them. God's Word gives us a guarantee that when any believer lays hands on the sick, they will recover:

> *"And these signs shall follow them that believe.....they shall lay hands on the sick and they shall recover."* (Mark 16:17, 18)

Jesus and others laid hands on sick people and got results (Acts 28:8-9; Matt. 20:30-34; Mark 6:5; Luke 4:40; 13:11-13). Jesus said that we would do the same works and even greater if we BELIEVE on Him (John 14:12).

You have the greater One living on the inside of you. The devil that is in the world is no match for the Greater One. When you lay hands on the sick and pray in faith the power of God that is IN you will flow OUT of you into the person's body. His power will overcome the devil's. When you lay hands on the sick remind yourself that the Greater One is living in you to manifest His power on the behalf of others.

5. Join Your Faith With Theirs

If the person that you are ministering to has weak faith then join your faith with theirs. You should be built up enough in God's Word to help strengthen the weak faith of another.

God tells us that when two or more are in agreement, heaven will move on their account:

> *"Again I say to you that if two of you shall agree on earth as touching ANY THING that they ask, IT SHALL BE DONE FOR THEM of my Father which is in heaven."* (Matt. 18:19).

When the sick one complains about the weakness of their faith then show them this Scripture. Let him or her know that they need not worry because you will join your faith with theirs. Both of you together can have strong enough faith to bring about the healing. The Bible shows us that two in unity can do ten times more than one individual (Lev. 26:7-8; Deut. 32:30). So join your faith with the sick one and watch the desired healing come to pass.

6. Use Your Authority

When ministering to the sick it is very important to know that Christ has given us authority over Satan and all his works. By using the name of Jesus we have the legal right to exercise authority over sickness and disease:

> *"Behold, I give unto you power to tread on serpents and scorpions, and over ALL the power of the enemy: and nothing shall by any means hurt you."* (Luke 10:19)

Notice that Jesus has given us power over ALL the power of the enemy. We know that Satan is the author of sickness and disease. Yet we have been given power over it. We should exercise this authority when ministering to the sick.

Some years ago our church had a hospital visitation program. Once a month we would go to the hospital and minister to the sick and pray for them. This one particular time some friends and I were going through a ward when we heard a woman moaning because of deep pain: "OOOOOOOOH! It hurts so bad!" We went straight to her room and asked her would she like for us to pray for her. She gave us permission so we grabbed hands and began to pray in the Spirit.

As we were praying the Holy Spirit told me, "Troy, command that spirit to come out of her stomach in Jesus' name." I then let go of my praying companions' hands. I pointed at her stomach and hollered, "Devil, get off that woman's stomach in the name of Jesus! Loose her and let her go!" After I did that she stopped moaning and with a surprised but pleasant look on her face said, "I feel so much better now."

Learn to exercise your authority and God will back you by His power.

7. Lead The Recipient To Exercise Their Faith

Lead the recipient to exercise his or her faith by praising and worshipping God. It is important for the person to do this in spite of any physical results.

A Syrophenician woman came to Jesus because of her daughter's sickness. She came begging and crying on her daughter's behalf. However, the Bible says that *"He answered her not a word."* (Matt. 15:23). When we pray and beg we may not get any answer from God.

Jesus further explained to her that he only came for the lost sheep of Israel. This would have been enough to discourage most Christians. They would have sadly walked away saying "I guess it's not God's will to heal me." Yet this woman would not give up. She tapped into the secret of receiving all of God's blessings:

> *"Then came she and worshipped him, saying, Lord, help me."* (Matt. 15:25)

She certainly received the Lord's attention after this, but again it seemed like a refusal. Yet she responded with determined faith:

> *"Then Jesus answered and said unto her, O woman, Great is thy faith: be it unto thee as thou wilt. And her daughter was made whole from that very hour."* (Matt. 15:28)

This woman demonstrated her faith by worship and determination. Jesus commended her and paid her the biggest compliment. He told her GREAT is thy faith. Jesus does not just mince words. He means what He says.

There are other accounts where worship was a part of receiving healing (Matt. 8:1-3). This is an action that is necessary to demonstrate one's faith.

Also make sure that the person makes the proper confession. Help them learn to confess the healing promises and not how they feel or even what the doctor says. Get them to speak only what God says and thank Him for it.

Again, God may lead you in a different way when ministering to the sick. We offer these principles only as guidelines for when you have not received a specific word from the Holy Spirit. God will honor His Word, your faith and that of the recipient. So go let God use you to heal.

Chapter Ten

Practical Wisdom And Divine Healing

"A false balance is abomination to the Lord: but a just weight is His delight." (Proverbs 11:1).

In this last chapter I want to deal with some practical issues concerning health. There have been extreme positions from both advocates and opponents of divine healing. I will attempt to deal with some of these areas as best as I can. I hope that this will help to deter some of the bondage that others have been subjected to because of the teaching of some ministers.

1. Healing And Doctors.

The Bible does not condemn doctors. The Bible does not even discourage us from consulting doctors. Doctors are not evil men and women. On the contrary there are good Christian men and women in the medical field. The Apostle Paul speaks of a physician with deep respect:

*"Luke, the **beloved physician**, and Demas, greet you."* (Col. 4:14)

Paul called Luke the *beloved physician*. Personally I believe that all of Paul's writings are given to us by the inspiration of God. I also believe that every jot and tittle in these writings are there for a purpose and for our benefit. This includes the greetings and the benedictions. There may seem to be no practical reason for Paul mentioning that Luke was a physician, especially a beloved one. However, if there may be only one purpose for writing this, it may be to show that doctors can maintain their practices and still be worthy servants of God.

Even our Lord Jesus Christ, while illustrating a point, mentioned doctors in a good light:

> *"But when Jesus heard that, he said unto them, They that be whole need not a **physician**, but they that are sick."* (Matt. 9:12)

No man has walked this earth who has had a greater healing ministry then the Lord Himself. Yet He recognized the need for doctors. He in no wise condemned them. Now we realize the context of Jesus statement. He was being criticized by the religious establishment of His time for fellowshipping with sinners. He used the sick and doctors to illustrate the need of the sinner to come to the only One who could deliver them.

However, If Jesus did not think well of doctors and felt that they were worthless then He would not have used them to illustrate His point. Doctors are not enemies of the church. Doctors are fighting against the same enemy that we are fighting. That enemy is sickness and disease.

Nonetheless, we are not encouraged to put our FAITH in doctors. King Asa is a good example of what happens when faith is misplaced:

> *"And Asa in the thirty and ninth year of his reign was diseased in his feet, until his disease was exceeding great: yet in his disease he sought not to the LORD, but to the physicians. And Asa slept with his fathers, and died in the one and fortieth year of his reign."* (2 Chron. 16:12-13)

Many preachers of faith and divine healing use this incident to condemn doctors. However, if we look at Asa's background then we will see that his death was not the result of going to the physician. It was the result of not seeking the Lord.

There are two Hebrew words used in the Old Testament that have been translated as "sought." The word used here is *darash*. This particular word is only used when referring to God or a false deity. *Wilson's Old Testament Word Studies* says this: " Often [used] of the pious, who habitually invoke God, to worship, to adore; spoken rarely of false gods, of whom their followers implore aid."{1}

You can see from the use of this word in the Hebrew that Asa was not just consulting the physicians or seeking medical attention. He gave these doctors the reverence, respect and trust that should only have been given to God. Asa was elevating the physicians to the level of godhood.

Asa started His career in faith (2 Chron. 14:2; 15:1-18). Later on though, Asa began to put more trust in MAN rather than God. God even sent a prophet to warn him of this (2 Chron. 16:7-9). Instead of Asa repenting of his sin, he had the prophet thrown in prison (2 Chron. 16:10). As we can see, Asa was putting more trust in men than in God. Therefore, Asa's consulting the physicians was not what hurt him. What destroyed Asa was giving the kind of TRUST to the physicians that should have been reserved only for God.

God does not want you and I trusting in anyone or anything except Him. He does not even want you and I to put our trust in PREACHERS. Does He condemn preachers? NO! He is the One Who calls them and raises them up. He is the One who anoints them for ministry. Yet, He wants us to trust Him and not them. In James 5:13-15, James instructs the sick one to call for the elders of the church to pray and anoint with oil. However, James is quick to remind us that the prayer of faith is what is going to save the sick, not the elders. It's faith in God, not in preachers. Yet the elders are men of God.

Therefore, just as God does not condemn preachers, neither does He condemn doctors. Many doctors are His servants but doctors are limited in what they can do. Let's look at one last incident in the Bible to see why God does not want us to rely on doctors:

> *"And a certain woman, which had an issue of blood twelve years, And had suffered many things of many physicians, and had spent all that she had, and was nothing bettered, but rather grew worse, When she had heard of Jesus, came in the press behind, and touched his garment. For she said, If I may touch but his clothes, I shall be whole. And straightway the fountain*

of her blood was dried up; and she felt in her body that she was healed of that plague. And Jesus, immediately knowing in himself that virtue had gone out of him, turned him about in the press, and said, Who touched my clothes? And his disciples said unto him, Thou seest the multitude thronging thee, and sayest thou, Who touched me? And he looked round about to see her that had done this thing. But the woman fearing and trembling, knowing what was done in her, came and fell down before him, and told him all the truth. And he said unto her, Daughter, thy faith hath made thee whole; go in peace, and be whole of thy plague." (Mark 5:25-34).

This woman went to doctors but got worse. Not only that, she spent her life savings. However, when she turned to Jesus, she was made completely well. The main reason God does not want you and I to put our TRUST in doctors is because they are limited in what they can do for us. God, however is unlimited.

There is no sin in consulting a physician. There are some who have grown so close to God and have received a revelation of divine health and therefore have no need of doctors. We are all at different levels of faith (Matt. 9:29). Do not feel guilty about seeing a doctor, but Trust God. If you must see a doctor ask God to give you wisdom as to which doctor to consult. Ask Him to give that doctor wisdom. As Him to guide the surgeon's hand and to bring about a supernatural recovery.

2. Healing And Medicine.

As with doctors, the Bible does not condemn medicine, but we are encouraged to put our faith in God. Medicine is made from the very elements that God placed on this earth for man's benefit:

"And God said, Behold, I have given you every herb bearing seed, which is upon the face of all the earth, and every tree, in the which is the fruit of a tree yielding seed; to you it shall be for meat." (Gen. 1:29)

These herbs and plants were placed on the earth for man's physical well being. I say this, not to promote the use of medicine, but to keep us from going to the extreme of condemning it.

God is not limited in how He heals. When Hezekiah was sick, they took a lump of figs and laid it on his boil but God did the healing (2 Kings 20:7; Isa. 38:20-21). God used a tree to heal bitter waters but reminded Israel that He was the Lord that heals them (Ex. 15:25-26). God instructed the elders of the New Testament church to anoint with oil but it is the prayer of faith that saves the sick and the Lord was the one to raise him up.

In other words, God is not beyond using means to bring about healing. Andrew Murray, in his book *Divine Healing*, makes this statement:

> "Does the use of remedies exclude the prayer of faith? To this, we believe our reply should be no, for the experience of a large number of believers testifies that, in answer to their prayer, God has often blessed the use of remedies, and made them a means of healing."

Yet Mr. Murray makes another statement earlier in his book:

> ".....when it is Jesus only to whom the sick person applies for healing, he learns to rely no longer on remedies, but to put himself into direct contact with His love and His almightiness."{2}

Mr. Murray neither advocates nor condemns medicine. What he encourages his readers to do is put their complete trust in the Lord Jesus Christ. If one's faith is not developed to the point that they no longer need medicine, then take medicine but trust God to do the healing. Pastor Frederick K. C. Price, in his excellent book, *How Faith Operates*, says this:

> "Remember that you are receiving your healing by faith. It is a matter of what you believe in your heart, or your spirit. Your heart, by faith, knows that you are healed, but your body doesn't know yet. Therefore, your body may still need

the medication. So go ahead and take it if you *need* it. All glasses and medication are doing is allowing the body to function at a normal level, until the physical healing is manifested in your body."{3}

Some things just make sense to do depending on the environment we are living in. Paul encouraged Timothy to take a little wine for his stomach's sake (1 Tim. 5:23). May I insert here the Paul was not giving the church a license to drink alcoholic beverages. This suggestion to Timothy was purely for medicinal purposes. Please do not use this passage to justify any weakness for alcohol.

We see from Timothy's situation as well as the other's that God neither advocates nor does He condemn the use of medicine. Nevertheless, the Bible recommends two kinds of medicine: God's Word (Prov. 4:20-22) and a merry heart (Prov. 17:22). These are the best medicines to take when we are in need of healing.

If you want to lose dependence on physical medicine, get into God's word and receive His joy. Start with the little things such as headaches and colds, then work upward. Do not wait until something serious comes along and then try to stand in faith without medical help.

3. Healing, Physical Exercise and a Proper Diet

.

Too many of God's people today are using the promises of divine healing as an excuse to neglect their bodies. Much, much, much sickness could be prevented if we properly took care of our bodies. Studies have proven that the many ceremonial washings and the declaration that some food and drink were unclean and forbidden were not instituted by God for religious purposes only. These were mostly for health purposes.

For example, in Leviticus 11:41-43 creeping and slithering creatures were forbidden to be eaten. These were snakes, lizards, frogs, rats, conies and other such. In Leviticus 11:1-8, animals such as pigs, camels and rabbits were forbidden. Today many dietitians will tell you that this type of food is not healthy for the body. These foods are the major cause of asthma, heart problems, and high blood pressure.

Other passages such as Leviticus 22:8 prohibited God's people from eating the meat of any dead animal that was killed by a wild beast or died of a disease. Anyone today with a little common sense knows how unhealthy this would be. Yet, this illustrates the truth that God was primarily concerned about the health and well being of His people.

I am not an expert on diet and I have no space to discuss proper diet here, but there are many good books on the subject today. There are even good Christian books that teach the biblical way of proper dieting and exercise. I highly recommend that you purchase and read these books.

The Bible is not silent concerning exercise, although it makes very little reference to it. 1 Tim. 4:8 is the closest reference to this:

"For bodily exercise profiteth little: but godliness is profitable unto all things, having promise of the life that now is, and of that which is to come."

Compared to godliness, bodily exercise profits little. Notice however that it does not say that bodily exercise *profiteth none*. There is a little profit in bodily exercise. As a friend of mine once said, "The Bible says that bodily exercise profiteth little, and you need all the little that you can get."

The major motivation for taking care of our bodies is the fact that our bodies are the temple of the Holy Spirit:

"What? know ye not that your body is the temple of the Holy Ghost which is in you, which ye have of God, and ye are not your own? For ye are bought with a price: therefore glorify God in your body, and in your spirit, which are God's." (1 Cor. 6:19-20)

In the Old Testament God held His people responsible for the building and maintenance of His temple. He rebuked His people when they neglected to fulfill their duty in this area (Haggai 1:3-11). I would imagine that God would feel stronger about the maintenance of His present temples than the building that was made from wood and stone (1 Cor. 3:16-17).

Many desire that God heal them of back aches, tiredness, etc. Even when God does heal these ailments they come back again due to slothfulness and ignorance. Take time to exercise. Eat properly. Do not fill the temple of God with a bunch of junk food. You will find yourself having to pray a whole lot less for healing and believing Him a whole lot more for divine health.

4. Healing And Action In Our Faith

"Even so faith, if it hath not works, is dead, being alone" (James 2:17).

When people first hear faith teaching, especially in the area of healing, they are quick to throw away their medication, eye glasses, etc. Later, they suffer the consequences of their hastiness. This is not always their fault since they are many times urged by some teachers of faith and healing to do so. Although we should demonstrate genuine faith, we must be careful about presumption and foolishness.

Christians should realize that there are *spiritual* realities and *physical* realities:

"Therefore I say unto you, What things soever ye desire, when ye pray, believe that ye receive them, and ye shall have them." (Mark 11:24)

Notice what Jesus says concerning faith. He tells you that you must first believe that you receive what you ask God for. In other words, when I ask God to heal my body I must consider it done. All of God's promises are present tense realities (2 Cor. 1:19-21; 2 Pet. 1:3-4). We believe that God has done it even when we do not see or feel it (2 Cor. 5:7).

The next statement is a promise: "ye SHALL have them." Jesus does not promise that what you ask God for will manifest right away. He only guarantees that it WILL happen as you stand in faith, believing that God is not a liar and that He will bring His Word to pass in your life.

The Word of God is "seed" (Luke 8:11). Give God time to cultivate the seed and allow it to grow (1 Cor. 3:6), Fruit will come (Luke 8:15). Don't throw away your medicine, wheel chair, crutches, glasses, or any other aids unless you receive a direct word from the Lord to do so. Don't do it just because a minister or any other well meaning Christian tells you. Remember what Pastor Price said: "Your heart, by faith, knows that you are healed, but your body doesn't know yet. Therefore, your body may still need the medication." {4}

There is a difference between healing by faith and the gifts of healing (1 Cor. 12:9). Gifts of healing are instant and require no faith. Healing by faith is through the word (Ps. 107:20). Stand on the Word regardless of your physical condition. Believe that God has healed you even when there is no physical evidence. Demonstrate your faith by praising and thanking Him for the healing. Speak His Word over your body. However, do not throw away any medication or other aids until you know that you are ready.

In conclusion, wisdom should be used in all areas of our life. If it is cold or raining, wear a jacket. Do not do foolish things to jeopardize your health in the name of faith and divine healing. Just as Jesus would not tempt the Lord just to prove the promises of divine protection (Matt. 4:5-7), neither should we do this just to prove we have faith for healing.

Appendix One

Promises For Healing

God's Word tells us, *"My son, attend to my words; incline thine ear unto my sayings. Let them not depart from thine eyes; keep them in the midst of thine heart. For they are life unto those that find them, and health to all their flesh."* (Prov. 4:20-22). Therefore, God's Word is the source in which we appropriate faith for healing.

When you are being attacked with sickness then meditate on the promises below. Confess them over and over again. Thank God for being true to His Word. When doubts come to your mind then read these Scriptures to Satan until he flees (James 4:7). Do this until you see the manifestation of healing in your body.

"Surely our sicknesses he hath borne, And our pains -- he hath carried them, And we -- we have esteemed him plagued, Smitten of God, and afflicted. And he is pierced for our transgressions, Bruised for our iniquities, The chastisement of our peace [is] on him, And by his bruise there is healing to us." (Isa. 53:4-5; Young's Literal Translation)

"When the even was come, they brought unto him many that were possessed with devils: and he cast out the spirits with his word, and healed all that were sick: That it might be fulfilled which was spoken by Esaias the prophet, saying, Himself took our infirmities, and bare our sicknesses." (Matt. 8:16-17)

"Who his own self bare our sins in his own body on the tree, that we, being dead to sins, should live unto righteousness: by whose stripes ye were healed." (1 Pet. 2:24)

"And said, If thou wilt diligently hearken to the voice of the LORD thy God, and wilt do that which is right in his sight, and wilt give ear to his commandments, and keep all his statutes, I will put none of these

diseases upon thee, which I have brought upon the Egyptians: for I am the LORD that healeth thee." (Exodus 15:26)

"And ye shall serve the LORD your God, and he shall bless thy bread, and thy water; and I will take sickness away from the midst of thee. There shall nothing cast their young, nor be barren, in thy land: the number of thy days I will fulfil." (Exodus 23:25-26)

"And the LORD will take away from thee all sickness, and will put none of the evil diseases of Egypt, which thou knowest, upon thee; but will lay them upon all them that hate thee." (Deut. 7:15)

"God will save you from hidden traps and from deadly diseases. He will protect you like a bird spreading it's wings over its young. His truth will be like your armor and shield. You will not fear any danger by night or an arrow during the day. You will not be afraid of diseases that come in the dark or sickness that strikes at noon." (Ps. 91:3-6; The Everyday Bible)

"A Psalm of David. Bless the LORD, O my soul: and all that is within me, bless his holy name. Bless the LORD, O my soul, and forget not all his benefits: Who forgiveth all thine iniquities; who healeth all thy diseases; Who redeemeth thy life from destruction; who crowneth thee with lovingkindness and tender mercies; Who satisfieth thy mouth with good things; so that thy youth is renewed like the eagle's." (Ps. 103:1-5)

"He sent his word, and healed them, and delivered them from their destructions." (Ps. 107:20)

"And he said unto them, Go ye into all the world, and preach the gospel to every creature. He that believeth and is baptized shall be saved; but he that believeth not shall be damned. And these signs shall follow them that believe; In my name shall they cast out devils; they shall speak with new tongues; They shall take up serpents; and if they

drink any deadly thing, it shall not hurt them; they shall lay hands on the sick, and they shall recover." (Mark 16:15-18)

"But if the Spirit of him that raised up Jesus from the dead dwell in you, he that raised up Christ from the dead shall also quicken your mortal bodies by his Spirit that dwelleth in you." (Rom. 8:11)

"For we which live are alway delivered unto death for Jesus' sake, that the life also of Jesus might be made manifest in our mortal flesh." (2 Cor. 4:11)

"My son, forget not my law; but let thine heart keep my commandments: For length of days, and long life, and peace, shall they add to thee... Be not wise in thine own eyes: fear the LORD, and depart from evil. It shall be health to thy navel, and marrow to thy bones." (Prov. 3:1-2, 7-8)

"Is any sick among you? let him call for the elders of the church; and let them pray over him, anointing him with oil in the name of the Lord: And the prayer of faith shall save the sick, and the Lord shall raise him up; and if he have committed sins, they shall be forgiven him. Confess your faults one to another, and pray one for another, that ye may be healed. The effectual fervent prayer of a righteous man availeth much." (James 5:14-16)

"Meats for the belly, and the belly for meats: but God shall destroy both it and them. Now the body is not for fornication, but for the Lord; and the Lord for the body. And God hath both raised up the Lord, and will also raise up us by his own power." (1 Cor. 6:13-14)

"What? know ye not that your body is the temple of the Holy Ghost which is in you, which ye have of God, and ye are not your own? For ye are bought with a price: therefore glorify God in your body, and in your spirit, which are God's." (1 Cor. 6:19-20)

"Ask, and it shall be given you; seek, and ye shall find; knock, and it shall be opened unto you: For every one that asketh receiveth; and he that seeketh findeth; and to him that knocketh it shall be opened. Or what man is there of you, whom if his son ask bread, will he give him a stone? Or if he ask a fish, will he give him a serpent? If ye then, being evil, know how to give good gifts unto your children, how much more shall your Father which is in heaven give good things to them that ask him?" (Matt. 7:7-11)

"And Jesus answering saith unto them, Have faith in God. For verily I say unto you, That whosoever shall say unto this mountain, Be thou removed, and be thou cast into the sea; and shall not doubt in his heart, but shall believe that those things which he saith shall come to pass; he shall have whatsoever he saith. Therefore I say unto you, What things soever ye desire, when ye pray, believe that ye receive them, and ye shall have them. And when ye stand praying, forgive, if ye have ought against any: that your Father also which is in heaven may forgive you your trespasses. But if ye do not forgive, neither will your Father which is in heaven forgive your trespasses." (Mark 11:22-26)

"O LORD my God, I cried unto thee, and thou hast healed me." (Ps. 30:2)

Why I Can Trust God For Healing

I know that it is the will of God to heal all that come to Him based on His promises.

Ephesians 6:9; Acts 10:34, 38; Matthew 8:16-17; James 5:14-15

I know that God desires to heal me more than I want to be healed.

Mark 1:40-41; 3 John 3:2; Psalm 35:27; Luke 12:32; Matthew 7:7; John 16:26-27

I know that Jesus was my substitute on the cross for my sicknesses as well as my sins.

Isaiah 53:4-5; Matthew 8:17; 1 Pet. 2:24; Gal. 3:13; Num. 21:9; John 3:14

I know that sickness is the result of sin that is in the world. The atonement of sin also covered sickness.

Genesis 2:17; Romans 5:12; John 5:14; Proverbs 3:7-8; Psalm 103:2-3; James 5:15-16

I know that Satan is the author of sickness and disease and Jesus has destroyed his works over my life.

Deuteronomy 7:15; Exodus 12:23; Job 2:7; Luke 18:16; Acts 10:38; 1 John 3:8; Hebrews 2:14

I know that I am in covenant with God and healing is my redemptive covenant right.

Deuteronomy 7:9, 12, 15; Galatians 3:16-17, 29; Luke 13:16; Matthew 15:21-28; Psalm 89:34; Exodus 15:25-26

I know that healing glorifies God and I want my Father and my Lord Jesus to be glorified in my body.

1 Cor. 6:19-20; Psalm 50:23; Luke 5:25-26, 43; 13:13-18; Acts 3:8-9; 4:4, 21-22; 5:14-16

Notes

Chapter Three

1. Pearlman, Myer Knowing The Doctrines Of The Bible, Copyright (c) 1937, 1981 by Gospel Publishing House, Springfield, MO 65802.

2. Simpson, A.B. The Lord For The Body, Copyright (C) 1996 by Christian Publications, 3825 Hartzdale Drive, Camp Hill, PA 17011. All rights preserved.

3. Strong, James. The New Strong's Exhaustive Concordance of the Bible, Copyright (C) 1984 by Thomas Nelson Publisher's.

Chapter Five

1. While I do not believe that it is ever God's will for anyone to be sick, there are instances in the Bible in which God is said to be the very agent of some sicknesses (Acts 13:11; Rev. 2:20-22) or one of his angels (1 Chron. 21:14-16; Acts 12:21-23) rather than a devil or demon. Yet, even in this, we must remember that, *"he doth not afflict willingly nor grieve the children of men."* (Lam. 3:3). On those rare occasions where God is said to be the agent of sickness, it is because He has done everything else and is left with no other recourse. However, simple repentance will deliver us from this "chastening." On the other hand, Satan afflicts most willingly but we have been given authority over him. One way or the other, sickness is to be resisted either by repentance of sin or by commanding the sickness to leave if it is not the result of sin.

2. Strong, James. The New Strong's Exhaustive Concordance of the Bible, Copyright (C) 1984 by Thomas Nelson Publisher's.

3. Fraser-Tyler, C.E. "The Sealed Book," an article written in the The Sunday Magazine, Guthrie, Thomas (Editor), London: Strahan & Co., 1872, p. 181

4. Rotherham, Joseph The Emphasized Bible, Bradbury, Agnew & Co., ©1902, p. 919

5. I believe that 99.9% of sicknesses are either attacks of Satan himself or the results of being in a fallen world where death is allowed to reign until this last enemy has been done away with (1 Cor. 15). Nevertheless, because of what I see in Scripture, I am careful not to limit sickness only to God's allowance. Scripture does show that .01% when God was the agent.

6. Henry, Matthew Matthew Henry's Complete Commentary on the Bible, E-Sword Edition.

7. Vine, W.E. Vine's Expository Dictionary Of Biblical Words, Copyright (c) 1985 by Thomas Nelson, Inc., Publishers.

8. Cho, Paul Yonggi. Suffering...Why Me? Copyright (c) 1986 by Paul Yonggi Cho, Bridge Publishing, Inc. 2500 Hamilton Blvd, South Plainfield, NJ 07080

Chapter Six

1. Webster's Ninth New Collegiate Dictionary, Copyright (c) 1986 by Merriam-Webster Inc.

2. Simpson, A.B. The Christ In The Bible Commentary Vol. 4, Copyright (C) 1993 by Christian Publications, 3825 Hartzdale Drive, Camp Hill, PA 17011. All rights preserved.

3. Roper, J.R. My Covenant Memorial Name: I Am, Copyright (c) 1993 by Revivals Of Deliverance, Inc. P.O. Box 42426, Portland, Oregon 97242-0426.

Chapter Seven

1. Vine, W.E. Vine's Expository Dictionary Of Biblical Words, Copyright (c) 1985 by Thomas Nelson, Inc., Publishers.

2. Ibid.

Chapter Ten

1. Wilson, William. New Wilson's Old Testament Word Studies, Copyright (c) 1987 by Kregel Publications, a division of Kregel, Inc., P.O. Box 2607, Grand Rapids, MI 49501.

1. Murray, Andrew. Divine Healing, Copyright (c) 1982 by Whitaker House, Pittsburgh and Colfax Streets, Springdale PA 15144.

2. Price, Frederick K.C. How Faith Works, Copyright (c) 1976 by Frederick K. C. Price, Ever Increasing Faith Ministries, P.O. Box 80011, Los Angelos CA 90099-4849

3. Ibid.

Invitation and prayer for salvation

To become a TRUE Christian One must be born again -1. John 3:1-7

We must be born of the water and the Spirit. This water is not speaking of water baptism but of the Word of God (1 Pet. 1:23; James 1:18; 1 Cor. 4:15; Eph. 5:25-27).

There is only ONE avenue into heaven and that is to be born again. Water baptism, church membership, religious duties, giving to the poor, living a moral life, taking the Lord's supper, being a member of a denomination, or an INTELLECTUAL reception (vs. a heart reception) of Jesus Christ cannot save you. You must be born again.

Are you born again? If you are not you will not spend eternity in heaven with Jesus Christ but instead you will enter into eternal damnation. I urge you to consider accepting Jesus Christ as your savior.

To be born again is very simple. You need only accept Jesus Christ as your Lord and Saviour. Why not give your heart to Him today. All you need to do is ask Him to come into your life. If you are not sure of how to do this here is a simple prayer to pray:

Lord Jesus

I ask you to come into my heart right now. You said in your word that if I confess you with my mouth and believe in my heart that God raised you from the dead then I will be saved (Rom. 10:9). I recognize that I am a sinner and I need your forgiveness and a change in my nature. I repent of all my sin. I know that all that come to you, you will not reject (John 6:37). Thank you for your for dying for me so that I can be born again. Thank you Father for Jesus. Thank you Holy Spirit for coming in to my life. AMEN.

You are now born again. It's that simple.

By the way, welcome to the family!

Invitation to receive the baptism with the Holy Spirit

<u>What Is This Baptism?</u> He is a Gift to be given to the believer - Acts 2:38. Every born again Christian has the Holy Spirit in them but not every Christian has received the BAPTISM (immersion) with the Spirit.

He is also a PROMISE that can be claimed - Acts 1:4 A promise implies something that one has a legal right to claim. You need not beg, plead, and do things to earn this blessing. He is a gift so it's free. He is a promise that is claimed by faith. He can be received AFTER one is born again - Acts 19:1-6.

Though it is better to ask God for this baptism in your own way, below is a prayer that may help you if you are at a loss as to how to ask:

Heavenly Father

The Lord Jesus promised that I can receive the baptism with the Holy Spirit with the evidence of speaking with other tongues. You promised that if I ask then I would recive exactly that which I have asked you for. Father I thank you in the name of your son Jesus and I yield myself to you Holy Spirit. Thank you for baptising me with Your Spirit.

Now just lift your hands and receive. Don't forget to share this blessing with others.

Printed in Great Britain
by Amazon